What Others

T0060984

Kathy Hardy has quite a gift for expressing her story, including difficult thoughts and feelings, in a way that goes straight to the heart. I know *Comfort* is going to bless many hurting people out there and lead to the healing of many hearts.

—Patricia Coon
Mother of three children

Helpful, encouraging, and uplifting for people who find themselves with a recently diagnosed child battling chronic illness. It's raw, it's edgy, and it's honest.

—Kylee Black
Founder
Spirit Sparkplugs

Kathy Hardy has written a beautiful, personal, and honest account of raising eight children, three of whom have cystic fibrosis, a life-threatening genetic disease of the lungs and digestive system. Through heartwarming (and heartbreaking) stories, prayer, and devotions, she shares her journey in ways that evoke a range of emotions for the reader, including sorrow, joy, respect, disbelief, awe, gratitude, and frustration. *Comfort* is a story of one Christian mother's heartfelt experience with CF and the struggles of faith and self in her roller-coaster ride of motherhood. This autobiographical book can serve as a mentor-on-paper and prayer book for those facing similar struggles. A valuable resource for parents of special-needs children in the Christian community, *Comfort* shows how the Christian faith and trust in God can alleviate the emotional challenges of this debilitating disease. Readers will find profound lessons of trusting God, finding wisdom from struggle, reflecting on their own lives, and appreciating health.

—Ana Stenzel, MS
Genetic Counselor
Lucile Packard Children's Hospital at Stanford
Adult with CF
Author of *The Power of Two: A Twin Triumph over Cystic Fibrosis*

This book has the potential to change the lives of parents and caregivers of children with chronic illness—and help the children too.

—John Vonhof
Author of *Fixing Your Feet*

Kathy Hardy offers an honest and inspiring portrayal of her life with children who have cystic fibrosis. Her clear voice is one we can relate to as she faces many challenging decisions at times of crisis. Grounded in her faith, she reminds us that we are not alone. Her words of comfort extend a hand to parents of chronically ill children and to all of us facing tough family health challenges.

—Carroll Jenkins
Executive Director
Cystic Fibrosis Research, Inc.

Kathy Hardy has poured her own life experiences as a mother into this tender but insightful—and largely unprecedented—book. If you have a chronically ill child and are willing to enter into the exhortations and comforts of God's Word, Kathy's book is for you.

—P. Andrew Sandlin
President
Center for Cultural Leadership

Kathy's incredible journey has been an inspiration to me for several years. She lives what she has written. She always has a bright smile on her face, even when heartaches surround her. Her book will be an encouragement to many hurting hearts.

—Phyl Stover
Mother of three children, one son in heaven
Pastor's wife

Comfort provides an inside look at a Christian family's journey with chronically ill children. As a health-care provider and now as a school nurse, I see that the author challenges health-care providers to reconsider some difficult ethical issues as well as more helpful approaches to serving these families. I recommend this to book to families as well as to those who serve them.

—Rhonda Farrell Peacock
RN, MS, FNP

Comfort

Comfort

Inspirations For Parents of Chronically Ill Children

You Are Not Alone

Kathy Hardy

TATE PUBLISHING
AND ENTERPRISES, LLC

Scripture quotations marked (NASB) are taken from the *New American Standard Bible*®, Copyright © 1960, 1962, 1963, 1968, 1971, 1972, 1973, 1975, 1977, 1995 by The Lockman Foundation. Used by permission.

Scripture quotations marked (NIV) are taken from the *Holy Bible, New International Version*®, NIV®. Copyright © 1973, 1978, 1984 by Biblica, Inc.™ Used by permission of Zondervan. All rights reserved worldwide. www.zondervan.com

Scripture quotations marked (NLT) are taken from the *Holy Bible, New Living Translation*, copyright © 1996. Used by permission of Tyndale House Publishers, Inc., Wheaton, Illinois 60189. All rights reserved.

This book is designed to provide accurate and authoritative information with regard to the subject matter covered. This information is given with the understanding that neither the author nor Tate Publishing, LLC is engaged in rendering legal, professional advice. Since the details of your situation are fact dependent, you should additionally seek the services of a competent professional.

The opinions expressed by the author are not necessarily those of Tate Publishing, LLC.

Published by Tate Publishing & Enterprises, LLC
127 E. Trade Center Terrace | Mustang, Oklahoma 73064 USA
1.888.361.9473 | www.tatepublishing.com

Tate Publishing is committed to excellence in the publishing industry. The company reflects the philosophy established by the founders, based on Psalm 68:11,
"The Lord gave the word and great was the company of those who published it."

Book design copyright © 2016 by Tate Publishing, LLC. All rights reserved.
Cover design by Dante Rey Redido
Interior design by Shieldon Alcasid

Published in the United States of America

ISBN: 978-1-68352-215-7
1. Family & Relationships / General
2. Family & Relationships / Children with Special Needs
16.06.09

To my husband, Tom,
who is walking this difficult parenting journey with me,
for believing in me, my writing, and this book project.

ACKNOWLEDGMENTS

Thank you to

Dione Michelsen and Lisa Greene,
who kept after me to write a book.

my children,
Kelsey, David, TJ, McKenna,
Jordan, Shannon, Lynnsey, and Nina,
for providing me with endless experiences to write about.

my grandma, Gladys Hersey, and friend Phyl Stover,
my Bible study friends,
and all my other prayer warriors
for supporting me at all times.

my first spiritual mentor,
Sherilee Sheffield Luevano,
for helping to set my feet on the right path.

my wonderful editor,
Christy Miller,
for doing a great job on the manuscript
and being so patient with this first-time author.

Special thanks to
Marie Andersen and Patricia Coon
for reading through an early edition of the manuscript
and making corrections and helpful suggestions.

Lastly, my fantastic writing mentor,
John Vonhof,
for steering me in the right direction
and making it all happen

and

Jesus Christ,
for blessing me with a life
beyond my wildest dreams.

Contents

INTRODUCTION

If you care for a child with medical issues or know someone who does, if you want to understand what life is like for your family or friends with a sick child, if you know of a child who has had a devastating injury resulting from an accident, this book is for you. It is a brutally honest book filled with raw emotions that come while dealing with chronic illness.

You may relate to the day-to-day challenges or simply gain more empathy for those you love. No matter what disease or condition the child you love is afflicted with, we who love and care for them share many of the same experiences. From the first symptoms, the diagnosis, the loss of hope, the change of dreams and plans, the struggle to overcome the challenges, the dealings with hospitals and medical staff, and on to death and dying issues, my hope and prayer is that you will say, "Yes, that is exactly how it feels! I'm glad someone else understands," or, "Oh, now I see what you have been going through."

> Praise be to the God and Father of our Lord Jesus Christ, the Father of compassion and the God of all comfort, who comforts us in all our troubles, so that we can comfort those in any trouble with the comfort we ourselves receive from God. (2 Cor. 1:3–4, NIV)

I hope you will feel comforted as you realize you are not alone in your circumstances. You have been specially chosen for this awesome assignment. It is an honor and privilege to be given such a precious gift: the raising of your chronically ill child. The short readings will not only help you sort out confusing feelings but will also equip you to explain them to others.

I have found daily journaling to be a great source of self-therapy with a calming influence. I encourage you to journal through your experience.

This book can be used many ways. It can be a guide for personal quiet times, a tool for families to share with friends or relatives to help them understand the experience of having a chronically ill child, or a book to read at support groups. It can be a gift to parents or loved ones of a child with a newly diagnosed condition or an aid for pastors and counselors dealing with a distraught family who has received an unwelcome diagnosis for their child. The book concludes with a resource section that specializes in children's diseases and a reading list of related books.

PREFACE

Who knew?

Who would *want* to know? I'm glad God didn't show me the future when I was a young bride. I surely would have said, "No thanks, God. I cannot manage all of that. I don't even want to try."

It's a good thing God didn't show me. It would have been beyond overwhelming. And unwelcome. And heartbreaking. However, just as a baby doesn't fully develop inside its mother's womb instantly, our family didn't just appear one day. It took years to grow into what it is today. And it also took all this time for God to grow me into the person I am today, fully reliant on Him to get through every minute of every day.

Tom and I met at a summer Bible study in 1979, shortly after my high-school graduation. We attended the same college and spent a lot of time together, working in the college bookstore and doing homework in the evenings. We became best friends and eventually realized the next step in our relationship was marriage. We were married in 1981.

Who knew?

Who knew we each harbored a defective gene, which was harmless alone, but if brought together would produce a child destined to live a life of hardship, suffering, and early death?

Who would want to know something like that? Not Tom and not me.

Our defective genes didn't come together only once to produce a child with a devastating disease. They came together three times.

Back in those carefree days, we were oblivious to the fact that our whole lives would be influenced by this "coming together." But a few years later, our family's focus took a turn down a road we didn't even know existed.

Tom and Kathy

K
E
L
S
E
Y

1

D-DAY AND BEYOND

Heart Psalm 1
The Diagnosis

A regular day.
A well-baby checkup.
The doctor scratches his head, confused.
Something is wrong.

What was that?
I don't understand what you are saying!
My knees go weak.
My blood turns to ice.
I need to sit down.

It can't be true!
That doesn't run in our family.
Or maybe it does.
I can't breathe.
I can't think straight.

Life has changed, forever,
without my permission.
An hour ago was *the before*.
This is *the after*.
Things will never be the same.

The Diagnosis: Devotional

I call on you, O God, for you will answer me;
give ear to me and hear my prayer.

—Psalm 17:6 (NIV)

Nothing has ever gotten my attention as quickly and profoundly as the diagnosis of our first sick kid. Life suddenly and permanently changed. I have been hitting the floor with my knees on a regular basis since D-day.

And that is good because otherwise, life may have become commonplace for me. I may have grown complacent and disregarded my daily dependence on God. But that is not likely to happen now. Now my reliance on Him is absolute, undeniably so. My child's diagnosis, subsequent treatments, and health improvements and declines have made me ever aware of my dependence on God.

Some people think God made my kid sick to get my attention. I don't necessarily believe that, but I know God has control over everything. He is sovereign. He could have prevented my child's illness if He had chosen to.

I sometimes wonder what our lives would be like if all our children were healthy. How would things be different? What would our children's lives look like? What would *my* spiritual life be like? Would I see the need to spend time with God each morning, imploring Him to direct my day and empower me to do His will?

God is God and does as He deems best without having to answer to me. I can't see the whole picture, yet He can. Each day, more is revealed. But for now, I see just a glimpse.

Do you sometimes wonder what God is doing? Do you question His methods? Does your child's illness challenge your faith? Take heart! You are not alone! It's okay to question and struggle. We all do. God knows and understands. But let us not stay in the quagmire of challenging God. He wants us to grow in our relationship with Him, and He is here to carry our burdens.

Dear God,

I really sat up and paid attention
when my child was diagnosed.
As I am getting past the shock, grief, and anger
and am coming to a place of
acceptance and gratitude,
please make me ever aware of Your presence and
never-ending loving-kindness.
Hear me when I pray, O God.
Thank You.

Amen.

Prayers, Notes, Reflections

_____

_____

_____

_____

_____

_____

_____

_____

_____

_____

_____

_____

_____

_____

_____

_____

_____

_____

_____

_____

_____

_____

_____

_____

Heart Psalm 2
Don't Miss the Blessing

Did I ask for this?
No.

Is this what I wanted?
Is this what I expected?
Is this what I bargained for?
No. No. And NO!

I wanted something different.
I wanted some*one* different.
I didn't mean *different*!

I just meant different from what I got.

This is too hard.
Won't the rest of my family suffer?
I can't do this!

How can I possibly manage?
How can I possibly raise this child?

Ah, finally, the right questions!
And the answers?

Only by the grace of God.
Only with God's love and strength.

Only with the wisdom God gives
to those who ask.

And with the help and support
from His family.

Don't miss out on a blessing
because it isn't packaged the way you expected.

Don't Miss the Blessing: Devotional

But if any of you lacks wisdom, let him ask of God,
who gives to all men generously and without
reproach, and it will be given to him.

—James 1:5 (NASB)

Not many of us would ask to raise a sick kid. However, I have met a few people who requested a health-challenged child when they were seeking to adopt. They are a rare breed of selfless people who desire to raise special children who, because of their illness, may not otherwise be adopted.

But most of us want a "normal" child. Most of us want a "perfect" baby. What is normal, anyway? What does perfect really mean?

The plain fact is, normal for my family isn't what's normal for your family. When it comes to looks, for example, you may think a blond-haired, blue-eyed baby is perfect. Someone else may prefer dark hair and eyes. Have you ever heard a conversation in which someone asks a newly pregnant couple if they want a girl or a boy? I just hate it when the couple says, "It doesn't matter, as long as it's healthy." Well, what if the baby isn't healthy? Are they going to give it back?

I may not know much, but this I *do* know: God knew what child was "perfect" *for me*. He knew what circumstances would be "perfect" to continue my character training and make me into a more useful vessel. And He knew which child would be perfect for you.

You may wonder why God blessed/cursed you with an ill child. You may feel overwhelmed, inadequate, not up for the task. But rest assured, God knows what He's doing. He will grant you all the strength, love, compassion, and patience you need to get through each day. All you have to do is ask, and keep on asking.

> Thank You, once again, Lord,
> for knowing more than I.
> For knowing what is best for me.
> When I think I know what is best, I just repeat:
> "There is a God and it's not me.
> There is a God and it's not me."
> I am so grateful that You have Your job, and I don't.
> Thank you endlessly for the blessing of my child.
>
> Amen.

Prayers, Notes, Reflections

_____

_____

_____

_____

_____

_____

_____

_____

_____

_____

_____

_____

_____

_____

_____

_____

_____

_____

_____

_____

_____

_____

_____

_____

_____

Heart Psalm 3
Character over Comfort

I want the easy life.
I don't like hardships.
Give me a life without difficulties.
Without worries.
Without cares.

But...
How could God use a person like that?
How attractive is a lump of coal?

I feel God putting me under pressure
to bring about the priceless jewel.

He is putting me through the fire
to purify me like gold.

It is not fun!

But God cares more about my *character*
than my *comfort*.

I dislike character-building experiences.
But I am grateful for them.

I am grateful that God loves me just as I am.
But He loves me so much,
He isn't content to leave me this way.

He is always working on me,
knocking off the rough edges.

I once heard that
You can't climb a mountain if the sides are smooth.

I want to see the view from the pinnacle.
So I have to work hard to climb to the top.

Character over Comfort: Devotional

And not only this, but we exalt in our tribulations,
knowing that tribulation brings about
perseverance; and perseverance, proven character;
and proven character, hope; and hope does not
disappoint, because the love of God has been
poured out within our hearts through the Holy
Spirit who was given to us.

—Romans 5:3–4 (NASB)

I WONDER WHAT kind of person I would be today if my child hadn't been born with his disease. What differences would be apparent in *him*? How would my husband be different? Our family?

Illness has had a definite impact on us all. We are different than we would have been. Before chronic illness appeared on our horizons, I didn't give God much of a thought throughout my day. Occasionally I would remember to talk to Him, mostly to ask for something. But now, I meet with Him early every morning and take Him with me as my constant companion throughout my day. We converse and confer about everything. I call upon Him when I face challenges and struggle with issues.

Hardships of many kinds have taught us many valuable lessons. The word *hardship* begins with the word *hard* for a reason. It is a hard road not many of us would choose.

But for whatever reason, this is the path God chose to develop our character. Character training is hard. It is not fun. But, oh, the rewards! The hardest tasks I've ever had to perform have brought me into a communion with God that I never imagined possible.

Isn't that just how God works?

When you face hardships, don't hesitate to talk to God. In fact, don't wait for the hardships to come along. God is crazy about you and desires to spend time with you every day. Try taking Him along with you as your constant companion and see how different your day turns out.

> Dear Lord,
>
> I must be honest. I don't like character training.
> It hurts. It takes too long.
> I sure like the rewards, the results, though.
> Please help me to be obedient,
> to seek Your will
> and set aside my own selfish desires.

After all, You know what's best for me, my child, my family, all of us.
Create a useful vessel out of me.
Thank You.

Amen.

Heart Psalm 4
Chosen

I did not choose
to raise and nurture
a "special" child.

It is so hard
and
I am not willing.

Why was *I* chosen
to raise and nurture
this special child?

The job is so demanding
and
I am not capable.

Wait! This child with a new diagnosis
is the same wonderful child
I have loved and nurtured
all along.

How did I get so lucky
~to be chosen~
to raise and nurture
a special child?

It is so challenging
but
I learn so much.

It is an honor
to raise and nurture
my special child.

It is so hard
but
there is such bitter sweetness
as I watch my child
live out his life purpose.

I don't understand why,
but he is also chosen.

Chosen: Devotional

The word of the Lord came to me, saying, "Before
I formed you in the womb, I knew you. Before you
were born, I set you apart; I appointed you as a
prophet to the nations."

Jeremiah 1:4–5 (NIV)

I am a contemplative person. Every breath I breathe, every
flower I see and smell, every bird I hear singing outside
my window is a miracle. The way every environment and
ecosystem on earth works together perfectly to sustain
human life is a miracle!

When my first baby was born, I sat holding her for hours,
gazing at her in wonder. I pondered the fact that just a
few short months earlier, this complete, beautiful, complex

child was a mere cluster of cells that divided and became specialized to forever perform specific bodily functions. It was a miracle! It is all a miracle!

This contemplative nature also leads me to wonder why I was chosen to live this life inundated by illness when my siblings weren't. Is it all just happenstance that I live in this wonderful country, in this neighborhood, in this house while others are born in war-ravaged countries or into gang-infested neighborhoods? Some families seem to be perfect or touched by fortune. Their children are all talented, beautiful, athletic, and intelligent. Things go their way, they get the perfect job, and they live in beautifully decorated houses in the "right" neighborhoods.

It leads me to wonder how these specific children came to be born to me. It is mind-boggling to imagine that it is all by design; it is all to accomplish God's purpose.

Wow!

Do you wonder how things happen in your life or the lives of others? Why your friends have "perfect" children or seemingly gifted lives? Do you find yourself being envious? I do, sometimes. But only for a second. I see my children as the wonderful reward, the blessing that I don't deserve, not the booby prize. Every moment that I begin to wonder or wallow is just the right time to get my eyes off my circumstances and turned back toward God.

Dear God,

Thank you for the privilege of knowing
these children You have entrusted to me.
Please strengthen me and grant me wisdom
to know just how to serve them
and also to receive the blessings
You give me in every situation.

Thank You.
Amen.

Heart Psalm 5
Mommy Guilt

I stand at the kitchen sink, washing dishes.
My four-year-old approaches and inquires,
"Mommy, do I have *sixty-five roses*
because I cried too much
when I was a baby?"

I am taken by complete surprise.

Shocked, I look down at the sweet, little, innocent face
of my beautiful child.

My throat chokes with a lump.
My eyes tear up.
My mouth goes dry.
My mind is blank.
My tongue gets tied.

"No, honey," I finally manage.
"You don't have *cystic fibrosis*
because you cried too much."

I confess the truth
about his inherited disease:
"Mommy and Daddy gave it to you,
but we didn't mean to.
We're really, really sorry."

Mommy Guilt: Devotional

You made all the delicate, inner parts of my body
and knit me together in my mother's womb.
Thank you for making me so wonderfully complex!
Your workmanship is marvelous—how well I know it.
You watched me as I was being formed
in utter seclusion, as I was woven together
in the dark of the womb.
You saw me before I was born.
Every day of my life was recorded in your book.
Every moment was laid out
before a single day had passed.

—Psalm 139:13–16 (NLT)

Our family members had to deal with their own feelings regarding our children's illness. Some felt guilty for passing on the defective gene. Most were profoundly sad and fell into a state of grieving. One became a full-time volunteer with a national organization that raised money for research to find a cure for our children's disease. This was a therapeutic reaction for him.

Years later, I discovered it was also a way of dealing with the resentment and bitterness he harbored toward me. The day is etched into my memory forever, the day he said to me, "When David dies, it will be very sad, but when TJ and McKenna die, it will be your fault. You will be the one hammering the nails into their coffins. You brought them into this world, knowing they could have this disease. You didn't know about it before David, but you had fair warning with the others."

As you might imagine, I was stunned, shocked, and aghast! Our relationship was mortally wounded. I was intensely hurt and eventually became angry. God had much work to do in my injured spirit. Many years went by before I could have a normal, caring conversation with that family member. Only on his deathbed did we clear things up and forgive each other.

In reality, I had nothing to do with our children having a disease. Neither did my husband. God put our children together cell by cell. In fact, He made His intentions for them before the beginning of the earth.

Do you ever feel guilty for your child's illness or feel responsible for his condition? God offers complete forgiveness where ever necessary. He will set you free if you just ask. I have found that accepting the situation brings the wonderful serenity and peace we all seek. Let God have his way with you to accomplish His purpose, both for you and your child.

> Thank You, God, for Your assurance
> that I did nothing wrong.
> In fact, I acted in obedience to You.
> You willed each of our children into existence
> to fulfill Your purpose, whatever it is.

It is not for me to question. You are God, and I am not.
Thank You for making, wonderfully,
each of our children.
Yes, I agree. Wonderful are Thy works!

Amen.

Heart Psalm 6
Suffering

I heard a mom talk about her sick child.
She described their daily routine.
She talked about the doctor team they visit.
She related the activities her child enjoys.

And then she said it...
the word that put a lump
in everyone's throat.

She said, "I thought I had
prepared myself for everything."
But," she continued,
"I wasn't prepared to see my child *suffer* like this."

Suffering.

The word is offensive.
It assaults the senses.

To watch a child suffer.

Who suffers more?
The child?
Or the parent who watches?

The parent who holds the trembling hand,
Who mops the feverish brow,
Who holds their hair back while they vomit.
Who spoons broth into the reluctant mouth,

Who restrains the child during a painful and
terrifying procedure.
Who attempts to calm a fearful spirit,
all the while struggling to believe
her own soothing words.

It is impossible to know
who suffers more.

Does it matter?

Really?

Suffering: Devotional

"Father, if you are willing, take this cup from me;
yet not my will, but yours be done."
An angel from heaven appeared to him and
strengthened him. And being in anguish,
he prayed more earnestly, and his sweat was like
drops of blood falling to the ground.

—Luke 22:42–44 (NIV)

Some things we just will never know, like why a child has
to suffer.

I feel pretty smug, so often thinking I have accepted
God's will for me, my sick child, and my family, thinking I
am managing pretty darn well. My morale is high, and I am

coping. And then I enter a period of crisis. Illness invades my territory.

I sit at my child's bedside, keeping vigil. I hold his hand, and I see pain contort the face of my loved one. I see uselessness in the pain. What purpose could it possibly serve? I watch him deteriorate and linger. He is suspended between this world and the next, and I wonder. Finally, I question,

Why, God?

Is this really necessary? What purpose could You possibly have in this? Could You make it me instead of him? Please, God, will You remove the pain from my suffering child? Or will You please just end it once and for all?

How could I have just thought that?

Will I be able to live the minute after my child leaves this earth? Can I possibly draw another breath when there is no more breath in my child?

The bedside-vigil questions continue. My heart is revealed in all truth. Where there was once serenity and confidence, there is now only doubt and fear.

I didn't really want to know this about myself.

What are you learning about yourself as you watch your child suffer? Do you doubt God's wisdom or compassion? Are you having a crisis of faith? Are you drawing closer to God, falling at His feet, pleading for the life of your child? Or are you begging for your child's comfort as he passes out of our world? God knows your heart. After all,

He watched His own beloved Son suffer. He is with you.
And He understands.

Dear God,

I am comforted as I recall
Jesus's prayers and petitions to You
from the Garden of Gethsemane.
It is perfectly human to question and to fear.
Thank You for walking along so close at all times,
but particularly when life is so scary.

Amen.

Our Story:
Let's Start at the Very Beginning

Our first child arrived after Tom and I had been married five years. During our first four years of marriage, we suffered from infertility. It's funny now, considering how large our family grew to be, but it held no humor then. Nevertheless, shortly after our fifth wedding anniversary, Kelsey was born. She was a big, healthy, ten-pound, ten-ounce girl—the apple of our eyes.

When she turned two, Tom and I entertained the idea of producing a sibling for her. At first, we couldn't imagine being able to love another child as we loved her, but soon we were expecting our second child.

David came into the world weighing a whopping twelve pounds and four ounces.

After delivering that huge baby, I exclaimed, "Whew, I'm sure glad the hard part is over."

The wise nurse, who stood near my head, prophetically said, "Oh, no, the hard part has just begun." How true that statement turned out to be.

David was a wonderful baby. He ate and slept as a baby should. The only thing different about him in comparison with our firstborn was that he didn't have regular bowel movements. He would go only about once a week. I mentioned this to the doctor at David's two-month checkup, but he had gained three pounds since his birth, so nothing much was said about it.

When the constipation issue continued, I called the advice nurse. I was told not to worry about it because "breast-fed babies typically go seven to ten days between bowel movements." When I called back after another week or two, they told me to try inserting a rectal thermometer to encourage the baby to bear down. That didn't work.

I'm sure they just thought I was a nervous new mom. After several calls to the advice line, I began to think that if nobody else was concerned about this problem, I shouldn't be either.

But between David's second and fourth month checkups, he pooped only three times. And at the four-month checkup, his weight hadn't changed since his last appointment. The pediatrician thought someone had made a mistake while recording his weight at the previous visit.

About this time, Tom's parents, who saw us regularly, told us they were worried about David. They said he didn't look healthy. They thought he looked thin and said I should supplement his breast feedings. They had been dubious about my nursing Kelsey, so I became defensive and ignored their comments.

In retrospect, while looking at David's baby pictures, Tom and I could see he looked terrible at five months. He was underweight and had dark circles under his eyes. He also slept more than his sister had, which I didn't see as anything to complain about. But he slept thirteen hours straight, then woke only to eat, and then went back to sleep again. Apparently he wasn't absorbing enough nutrition to give him energy to do anything but breathe and sleep.

At David's six-month checkup, he had lost weight. Now the red flags popped up. The doctor scratched his head and tried to rework the math but couldn't reconcile the numbers. He began to worry. As he excused himself from the room, I became anxious.

When the doctor returned fifteen minutes later, he gave me a referral for a sweat-test screening. He solemnly said, "I'm having David tested for cystic fibrosis [CF] because of the symptom of *failure to thrive.*" A dreadful chill went up my spine. I had to sit down before I fell over.

The only thing I knew about CF was that one of our college bookstore coworkers had the disease. He coughed all the time, and he was pale and thin. I remembered talking about him to a friend of mine who was a nurse. She told me CF was fatal.

When the doctor told me cystic fibrosis was the first thing he wanted to test David for, I wanted to punch him in the nose. I wanted him to think of something else, *something less serious*, that could account for David's symptoms, something like celiac disease.

In the years to come, I heard several doctors commend David's pediatrician for thinking of the right diagnosis straightaway.

So because people with CF have a higher concentration of salt in their sweat, a sweat test was scheduled for David for the next day to aid in his diagnosis.

When we arrived at the hospital, the nurse attached a round sticker with wires coming out of it to the inside of David's forearm. The wires led to a tiny, portable machine that would stimulate his glands to secrete sweat. The sweat would collect in a tiny coiled tube under the sticker.

The process would take about an hour, so Kelsey and I took David next door to a Dairy Belle to get an ice cream cone. It was probably the first time in my life that I passed up a sweet treat. My emotions were in turmoil. I was walking around in a state of shock, not believing what was happening.

We went back to the doctor's office at the appointed time. They took the collected sweat to the laboratory to be analyzed, and we drove home to wait for the doctor's phone call.

One of the most extraordinary days of my life happened a few days later, when the doctor called with the test results. It was the closest I have ever come to giving in to despair. However, I consider it the most astonishing and remarkable of all my life experiences. It cemented my resolve and gave me a new direction for the remainder of my life.

When the phone rang, it filled me with dread and trepidation.

The doctor was on the other end. "I'm sorry to tell you this, but David's sweat test came back positive. David has cystic fibrosis."

My head spun. I feared I would faint.

The doctor had made a four-hour consultation appointment for Tom, David, and me. The next day, we were to meet with a pulmonologist in Oakland to begin learning about this terrible disease.

He'd also made an appointment for both David and Kelsey in a different facility in Oakland. There they would do a confirmation sweat test on David and a screening test on Kelsey, as a sibling of a newly diagnosed CF patient.

We would later find out that Kelsey's sweat test came back negative, thank God! And David's test came back positive, as expected.

I hung up the phone, shocked and stunned. I knew Tom would call me soon to find out whether the doctor had phoned yet. I went to David's room and picked him up. I felt a desperate need to hold him close. For the next three hours, I carried David around our apartment until my arms ached. I cried and paced and paced and cried. I prayed. I called out to God. I wondered what this all meant. *What will happen to our family? What will happen to David?*

When I could not physically hold my precious, sleeping, *sick* baby any longer, I staggered into the nursery and over to his crib. As I laid David down, I looked at his precious face and pondered aloud, "God, what am I gonna do?"

At that moment, I heard a voice. *Don't worry about his physical body. Your job is to teach him about Me.*

The voice may not have been audible, but the message was clear. It snapped me, instantly, out of my fearful and self-pitying stupor. Immediately my tears dried up. My mind cleared. And although I'd need to be reminded many times in the years to come, I knew then that somehow everything would be okay.

I had been given my marching orders. My job was to teach my child, my children—*all* children—about the saving grace and love of Jesus Christ.

We all get marching orders from God. Some take us up to the mountaintops, others through hot, dry valleys. Wherever we go and whatever burdens we carry, it's never a solo journey. Not only does God walk with us, but he prepares us for a purpose bigger than ourselves.

Before Diagnosis

D
A
V
I
D

More David

Prayers, Notes, Reflections

2

A WHOLE NEW WORLD

Heart Psalm 7
Precious Moments

Emergency rooms
Examination rooms
Hospital rooms
Waiting rooms

These are the places
where my sick child and I
have truly bonded
during our most precious moments.

We have had intimate conversations
about what matters most.

We have laughed the hardest
at silly, junior high humor.

We have cried together
when hearing an unwelcome prognosis.

When all seems lost
and good cannot be found
in the midst of crisis
caused by dreaded disease,
look for the silver lining.

Be grateful for the relationship.
Be thankful for the precious moments.

Precious Moments: Devotional

There is an appointed time for everything...A
time to weep and a time to laugh.

—Ecclesiastes 3:1, 4 (NASB)

We are anxious as we wait in the examination room for the doctor to arrive. My son, David, is having trouble breathing. We suspect a collapsed lung. To break our boredom, we begin an impromptu competition game. Since my child's disease involves two disgusting bodily fluids, namely, poop and mucus, we decide to list as many words as we can think of relating to them.

We begin with *A* and move on down through the alphabet. Some words are silly; some are naughty, which is extra funny since we don't normally use those words in our family. And when we can't think of a word for a particular letter, we make one up.

We laugh uproariously, which is intolerably painful for my child, who is experiencing such terrible lung discomfort, so we try to restrain ourselves.

And then it happens. The phlebotomist enters to draw blood from an artery in my son's wrist. He has never had an arterial blood draw before. He is in pain, scared, and tired. After all, it is the middle of the night, and we have been waiting for hours. The phlebotomist inserts the needle into the inside of my child's wrist and wiggles it around to get it placed properly. My son cries out. The phlebotomist says to my fourteen-year-old child, "Don't be such a baby."

I am angry at his horrendous bedside manner. I am in tears as I commiserate with my child's pain, but I nearly bust a gut when I hear David mutter under his breath, "I have twenty-six words for *you*."

Have you experienced such precious bonding moments with your sick child in the midst of pain and fear? Keep your eye out for such times. They present themselves when you look for them. They are a true gift. I don't think families of well children are blessed in the same way we are, or maybe we just have more opportunities to notice.

> Thank You, God, for precious, silly moments
> with our precious children.
> Please help caregivers and medical staff
> to remember that their patients are people, too.
> Help them to be patient and kind.
> Thank You.
>
> Amen.

Prayers, Notes, Reflections

_____

_____

_____

_____

_____

_____

_____

_____

_____

_____

_____

_____

_____

_____

_____

_____

_____

_____

_____

_____

_____

_____

_____

_____

_____

_____

_____

_____

Heart Psalm 8
Hospital Time

The doctor writes orders for a hospital admittance,
and immediately, time alters.

A bubble forms around us. It is called hospital time.

Before we even get to the hospital,
the space-time continuum has shifted.

Time slows down on the inside of our bubble,
but it stays the same on the outside.

Life on the inside becomes all about
health and wellness.
Life on the outside goes on without us in "normal time."

It's a strange phenomenon…
to move about at one speed
while watching people outside my child's
hospital room window
moving about at another.

Resentment nudges around the edge of my mind.
I don't want life to pass me by.
Or my child.

Especially my child.

And then time passes,
medications have been administered,

treatments have been performed,
and we are ready to be discharged.

As soon as the papers are signed,
even before leaving the ward,
the space-time continuum shifts back to normal.

We join back together—hospital time and
normal time become one.
Time is just time.
There is no difference anymore.

We go on with life.

Hospital time has ended.
Until next time.

Hospital Time: Devotional

This is the day which the Lord has made;
Let us rejoice and be glad in it.

—Psalm 118:24 (NASB)

Since our children were entering the hospital for IV
antibiotics at least two times per year, it made good sense
to get them each a portacath. This way, they avoided having
sedation, which can be taxing on their respiratory systems,
each time they got a PICC line. Of course, they didn't *want*
to have surgery, but, in the future, they would understand
how practical it would be. The kids had to fast during the

night and were not served breakfast on the morning of the procedure. We decided to do them one after the other and just get it all over with.

McKenna was first. She was teary, which is her typical modus operandi. I accompanied her to the preparation room, where we met the surgeon, and she explained the procedure to us. I stayed with McKenna until they rolled her gurney down the hall to the operating room.

By that time, TJ came rolling in to the preparation room, so I waited with him and signed the necessary paperwork. When the nurses came to get TJ, I kissed him good-bye and went to the recovery room to be with McKenna. Her procedure had gone fine, and I was just waiting for her to wake up.

McKenna was in pain when she finally opened her eyes. I asked the attending nurse for some pain meds for her. She got a measure of relief but was still quietly crying. Soon she was ready to go back to her room. We headed out to the elevator with a nurse pushing McKenna's gurney.

On the way to the bank of elevators, we passed the preparation rooms, and I saw David through one of the windows, so I headed in to say good-bye to him and sign the required forms. When I left him to go back to McKenna's side, an unconscious TJ was wheeled by on his way to the recovery room.

Where was I to go? Should I stay with David, as he was nervous about the impending procedure? Should I accompany the upset McKenna to her room? Or should I go with TJ to recovery? It was kind of comical as I pointed at each child in turn and said to the nurses, "That one is mine, and that one is mine, and that one is mine…What should I do?"

Do you ever feel stretched and pulled in different directions? Take a breath and send up a quick prayer, asking for direction and grace. God is with you and your child.

> Wow, God.
> Sometimes life really feels out of control.
> It's as if I'm operating at a different speed than the rest of the world.
> Please help me to slow down and make the wisest decisions for each circumstance
> and to forgive myself when I get it wrong.
> Please comfort my children
> during each part of their day,
> especially when life gets scary
> or unpredictable for them.
> Thank You, most precious God.
>
> Amen.

Heart Psalm 9
The Lost One

It's hard to believe,
but it's true.

It's been seven years since my miscarriage,
and I can't even remember
what the due date was supposed to be.

I still think of the night it happened,
but it doesn't sting like it used to.

I remember the details:
the blood,
the drive to the emergency room,
the Tupperware in my backpack
that held "the little one," and
the trip home in the middle of the night.

I remember the next day, thinking,
I just had a baby.

True, it wasn't alive,
but I had given birth.
I still had the cramps and bleeding to remind me.

But where was the reward?

Time heals all wounds.

It seems to be true.
We can heal,
but we will never forget

the lost one.

The Lost One: Devotional

The Lord is near to the brokenhearted.

—Psalm 34:18 (NASB)

In the midst of such a devastating loss, I was aghast to think I could still find humor in the dark corners of a sad situation.

While questioning me in the emergency room examination area, the nurse asked, "What makes you think you had a miscarriage?"

What makes me *think*? Huh?

I answered as honestly as I could. "Well, the baby in the Tupperware in my backpack on your counter over there gave me my first clue."

Is that sick or what?

In the long run, I believe a lot of what helped me heal was the fact that I was pregnant again before the lost baby was due to arrive, that the miscarriage wasn't the last chapter of my childbearing years.

I know it doesn't happen that way for every couple, though. If you have suffered a miscarriage and are still hurting from the loss, ask God to comfort you and to crowd close to you. He will heal your broken mommy (or daddy) heart.

Dear God,

Please be close to those who are brokenhearted.
We know that You created and love
the lost babies, too,
much more than we do, as hard as that is to believe.

Comfort us as we grieve.
Help us accept Your plan for our lives,
whether or not children are to be a part of them.

Thank You for Your everlasting love and kindness.

Amen.

Prayers, Notes, Reflections

Heart Psalm 10
Take a Vacation

I've heard the advice:
"Get away from it for a while—
a weekend, or an afternoon, even an hour.
Just get out of the house and take a break from your
child's disease."

It is impossible.
The disease is a part of me
because it is a part of him.
My child.
And I cannot forget,
do not want to forget about him even for an evening.

When I am away from him,
And I hear someone cough,
it is my child.
I hear the beeping of a truck as it backs up,
and it is my child's monitor alarming.

The disease is a part of me.

It is true; I can escape the routine of it all
for a few hours or days.
It brings temporary relief
and perhaps a measure of rejuvenation.

But it also brings guilt.

Because no matter how much *I* want it to be so,
no matter how much *he* wants it to be so,
my child cannot take a vacation from his disease,
no matter how hard we all try.

It permeates every cell of his body.
He cannot take off the disease
like it is a skintight full-body suit.
Just unzip it and hang it up in the closet
and come back after a while to put it back on.

It is impossible.
It is unfair.
It is heartbreaking.

Take a Vacation: Devotional

"For I know the plans I have for you,"
says the Lord.
"They are plans for good and not for disaster,
to give you a future and a hope."

—Jeremiah 29:11 (NLT)

While on a Make-a-Wish trip, our family learned an important lesson about vacations that involve children: while away from the comforts and safety of home, anything can happen. That usually includes illness and accidents.

When we arrived in our hotel room on the first day, our six-year-old little boy, TJ, developed a horrendous stomachache. He doubled over and screamed for several hours. I was on the phone, trying to reach our doctor team back home, while Tom was trying to figure out how to get to a drug store since we did not have the use of a car.

I finally reached the nurse. She suggested we give TJ an enema since it sounded as if he was terribly constipated. We prayed the condition didn't develop into a full-blown bowel blockage. Tom found a store that had the necessary products, and after several hours, TJ felt well enough to continue with our plans to go to the park.

On the third day of our trip, TJ felt terrible again. He was low-energy and had a fever. We decided to go to Knott's Berry Farm, anyway, as planned. We were doing the best we could to keep our five children from running in different directions, as they all had different ideas of what would be fun. After developing a plan of action, we noticed we were missing one child. Where was TJ? We backtracked and looked all around the children's area, but we couldn't find him anywhere. I pictured him kidnapped or sick somewhere. I was beginning to get really worried.

As Tom and I were about to notify security, I heard an angelic little voice say, "Hi, Mom."

Who was that? Where was it coming from? Was I imagining it?

"Hi, Mom."

Again, I looked around and saw nothing.

"Up here, Mom."

I looked up and saw a sweet, happy, feverish face looking down and waving at me from high above us. TJ had wanted to go on the Ferris wheel, but in all the hubbub of trying to appease everyone, he must have decided, *This is my Make-a-Wish trip, so I'll just go on this ride while the rest of you make up your minds.* So that sick little six-year-old guy stood in line all by himself and rode the Ferris wheel. I was angry but relieved.

And I thank God I had the presence of mind to let him enjoy his happiness. I gently scolded him when he got off the ride, just enough to let him know how worried we were when we couldn't find him.

Have you encountered unplanned events or emergencies on a vacation? Take it as a reminder to connect with God. Take a deep breath and pray.

> Thank You, God, for *real* family vacations.
> Even when they don't turn out the way we plan,
> there are always lessons we can learn.
> Give us wisdom to see them and learn.
> Thank You.
>
> Amen.

Heart Psalm 11
Caregiver, Take Care

Without us,
what would they do?

Who would cook,
who would clean,
who would shop,
transport children to all their activities?

Who would coordinate
doctor's appointments?
Inventory and order medications?

Who would run the house
and care for everyone in it?

No one, that's who.

So we need to care for ourselves
so we can be there for everyone else.

We need to sleep as much as we can
and grab a nap whenever possible.
Eat properly, exercise.
Take care of our spiritual health.
Do something each day to nurture our soul.

Dance
Read
Journal

Cross-stitch
Take a walk
Scrapbook
Listen to or play music
Marvel at the sunrise or appreciate a sunset
Go out to the garden and smell and admire the flowers
Offer a prayer of thanksgiving.

Whatever it is that works for each of us,
we must do it!
Devote one half hour of each day to ourselves.

Caregiver, take care!

Caregiver, Take Care: Devotional

> And let us run with endurance
> the race God has set before us.
>
> —Hebrews 12:1 (NASB)

Have you noticed that flight attendants always instruct us to put the oxygen mask on ourselves before putting it on a child or elderly person in our care, should there be an emergency?

As caregivers to others, we need to take good care of ourselves first. But since our time is at a premium, here are some suggestions for finding moments for the things that nurture you:

❖ Always carry the book you are currently reading. If you get in a long line at the grocery store, doctor's office, post office, or pharmacy, you can read a page or two.

❖ While you are on hold on the phone, you can crochet, knit, or cross-stitch. If you are like me, you will more likely be loading the dishwasher or folding laundry.

❖ When you are ready to go somewhere and your family needs an extra fifteen minutes, assemble a page of your scrapbooking or pull a few weeds from the garden.

Find what nurtures you and then find a way to work it into your busy schedule. Oh, and here're three other ideas: (1) If someone offers help, take it! (2) If you have time for a nap, take it! (3) It is worth getting up fifteen minutes early to begin your day with Bible reading and prayer. Journaling is good and therapeutic, too.

Taking care of yourself physically, mentally, spiritually, and emotionally allows you to be available to care for others.

And remember, breathe.

> Dear Lord, please be with me as I care for others.
> Please help me to be kind and loving to myself.
> Thank You.
>
> Amen.

Prayers, Notes, Reflections

Heart Psalm 12
It's All Good

How often have I said,

"It's a *bad* day."
"This is *bad* weather."
"We got a *bad* report from the doctor."
"I feel *bad*."

All these things may *seem* bad.
I may *feel* bad.

But it's all relative.

If I believe the Bible,
and I do,
and it says that God is good
and has a purpose for everything and everyone,
and it does,

then it's all good.

It may not *feel* good.
I may not *understand* why God wills a certain thing.
I may not *agree* with Him.
I may not *like* it.

But none of those things change the fact that
God is good and only does good.

Even when I don't see it,
it's all good.

It's All Good: Devotional

And we know that God causes all things to work
together for good to those who love God and are
called according to His purpose.

—Romans 8:28 (NASB)

Gas prices in my town are $4.21 per gallon. Is that a "good" price? It all depends on your perspective. If this was the year 1960, we would all agree that $4.21 was a "terrible" or "bad" price, but this time last year, the price of gas was $4.89 per gallon, so today I would say, yes, $4.21 is a "good" price for gas.

It's all relative.

If you have a flat tire on the way to the airport and miss your flight, you would say the flat tire was a "bad" thing. But if you later learned that your scheduled flight had crashed, you would say the flat tire was a "good" thing.

My friend told me that her cancer was a wake-up call for her to return to her faith, so to her, her cancer was "good."

We don't see the whole picture. Only God does. It is a challenge to trust Him *completely*, but the Bible tells us God is loving and faithful, so I know I must try to trust Him.

How can disease, suffering, and painful death possibly be good? I don't know. I only know that God never leaves us. And there is a purpose in it. I may never know what it is. I just know I must trust God because He is good—all the time.

Dear God, please help me to trust You today
no matter what,
whether or not I feel like it,
even when it is hard,
even when I don't understand why.
Thank You.

Amen.

Our Story:
Our Family's Continuing Story

Our doctors, family members, and even complete strangers urged us to take permanent measures to avoid having more children, but we live by a higher authority than all of them, so we went on to have several more children. We stopped only when Tom and I both heard God telling us to.

After David's diagnosis, we somehow got through the next few days. We walked as if in a haze. The information we were supposed to absorb was cumbersome, technical, scientific, and foreign. A part of us rebelled. We didn't *want* to learn about all this stuff. We were not equipped to become a part of this new world of sickness. We wanted our old life back. We wanted normalcy. *This* didn't feel normal. But it was to become our *new normal.* This was our life, like it or not. We had joined a club that nobody wants to belong to.

These were the highlights we had to learn: CF has to do with the endocrine system. Anywhere there is mucus in the body, primarily the lungs and pancreas, will be affected. Basically, it affected eating and breathing, the two things we need to do to stay alive. This was not a good thing.

In the lungs, the mucus is supposed to be thin and slippery so it can catch dirt and germs. Then the cilia move them toward the larger airways to be coughed up and expelled from the body.

But in a person with cystic fibrosis, the thickened mucus traps the dirt and germs, which causes lung infections. This leads to more and more areas of the lungs becoming scarred. Then the air sacks can't be utilized, so the lungs become less and less useful over time.

In the pancreas, the abnormally thick mucus clogs the passageways through which the digestive enzymes are supposed to travel to reach the intestine, where the digested food is absorbed, so the person with CF doesn't grow properly. With the aid of enzyme therapy (enzymes made from pig pancreases), people with CF have been able to grow to a more normal size, and supplemental vitamins can improve overall health.

Ninety-eight percent of males with CF are sterile because of withered vas deferens. The news isn't much better for girls, as the thickened mucus in the reproductive tract is prohibitive to fertilization.

These facts were just the tip of the iceberg of what we needed to learn. Oh, and the doctor seemed pretty excited that the survival rate of newly diagnosed children had risen from twelve years of age to eighteen and recently had reached twenty.

Great, just great.

At his diagnosis at age six months, David was prescribed pancreatic enzymes, a mixture of amylase, protease, and lipase, to help him digest food. I opened the capsules and poured the granules directly into his mouth before I nursed him. The little granules rubbed me like grains of sand, very painful. But in the first week of his treatment, David gained seventeen ounces and grew more than an inch. In no time at all, he once again became a chubby, adorable baby. The enzyme therapy worked miracles.

And miracles were what we were seeking. We thought that if we prayed hard enough and had enough faith, God would heal David, so we had a little healing ceremony at our church. The pastor anointed David's head with oil, and we prayed fervently, but time would tell that a healing wasn't in the cards for our family. At least, it wasn't evident—yet.

In the next month or two, our little family began to create a new rhythm. We began to take the weekly "weigh-in" doctor appointments in stride. And we learned always to have extra diapers and to keep one bottle of enzymes with us in the diaper bag, one in the car, and one at Tom's parents' house.

David was only ten months old when I found myself pregnant again. TJ was born in January of 1991. He weighed eight pounds, ten ounces. His doctor sent a blood sample to a lab to be tested for CF. A week later, it came back negative. Hurray!

We took a weeklong vacation later that year when TJ was almost seven months old. My sister, Teri, let us stay at her house at Lake Tahoe for several days. Then we all drove over the mountain to our dad's huge new cabin outside Bridgeport for our stepsister, Nina's, wedding.

It was early August, and the weather was pretty hot. TJ seemed out of sorts much of the time, and he didn't feed well. I thought it was because he was cutting his first few teeth. The day after we returned home from the wedding, TJ had a well-baby checkup. It turned out to be anything but.

The same pediatrician who had diagnosed David was checking TJ out. He told us TJ had lost weight, and he was malnourished and dehydrated. TJ was admitted into the hospital posthaste and retested for cystic fibrosis. I felt as if I had been catapulted back into the same nightmare I had recently awakened from.

Can this happen again? I reflected with trepidation.

Making the phone calls to Tom, his parents, my mom, and my dad was horrible. All the parents said the same thing. "Perhaps this is a sign that you should get your tubes tied."

I wanted to scream! Because I was raised with the belief that you don't sass your elders, I couldn't say what I really felt, which was, "We don't obey or disobey God depending on our circumstances or on a whim. God hasn't told us to stop having children, and this event isn't going to sway us in the least." I didn't know how to speak my mind tactfully at that point in my life, so I just said, "We'll think about it."

While TJ's test result was pending, he was started on IV fluids, some kind of high-calorie oil, and enzymes. And of course, his test came back positive. We were to find out at a later date that we were one of three families that had received a *false negative* CF test result from that laboratory back in January of that year. Our pulmonary specialist was furious. The children's health suffered for more than six months, unnecessarily.

So now there were two.

Well, Tom and I thought, *at least we know what is wrong and how to treat it. Been there, done that.*

I was pregnant just two months later. This was not going to be a happy announcement for our families!

My fourth pregnancy progressed normally, with no problems besides the customary, debilitating morning sickness. During this pregnancy, I was introduced to the idea of having prenatal testing. There was a procedure called CVS, in which they go in through the cervix, snip a little piece of the placenta, and test it for CF. It has a 3 percent miscarriage rate, however, whereas amniocentesis (which tests for other anomalies) has a 0.5 percent miscarriage rate.

We were interested in neither test. The results of the tests would have no bearing on our decisions regarding continuing the pregnancy, and if the tests were positive, nothing could be done to help the baby until it was born anyway, so we opted to wait until the baby was delivered to do the testing. We continued this practice with our subsequent pregnancies. A little ignorance went a long way with us.

With Tom by my side yet again, I gave birth to McKenna on March 16, 1993, with the help of a wonderful midwife. McKenna was only eight and a half pounds and eighteen inches long, my smallest baby to date. Before I left the hospital the next day, the nurse took a blood sample and whisked it off to the lab for testing.

By this time, the genome project had mapped out the entire DNA strand, so they knew where to look for the major cystic fibrosis genes. David and TJ had been genotyped, and the lab knew that they needed to look for a double delta F508. Well, they found it. McKenna was diagnosed positive for cystic fibrosis at one week old.

And now there were three.

Prayers, Notes, Reflections

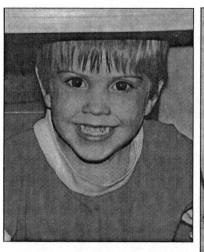

T
J

More TJ

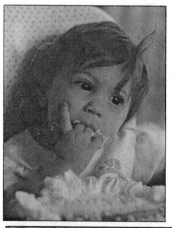

McKenna

More McKenna

Prayers, Notes, Reflections

3

GETTING ON WITH THE BUSINESS OF LIVING

Heart Psalm 13
Inside My Kid's Skin

How does my child feel?

I don't mean his emotions.
But how does he *really* feel in his body?

Is he in pain?
Does he *really* have a stomachache
like he says he does?
Does his head *really* hurt?
Are his joints *truly* sore?

I have no way of knowing.
I can't crawl inside of my kid's skin
to really find out what is true.

I have to rely on his word.

Should I keep him home from school?
Write a note to excuse him from PE?

How does he feel?
Why would he lie?

Well…maybe I *should* consider his emotions.
How does he *feel?*

Is he sad? Melancholy?
Afraid? Confused? Angry?

He has every right to be all of these
…and more.

But how do I know for sure?

Even if I *could* find out,
what could I do to help?

We could talk about it.
But that wouldn't change the facts:
He still has what he has.
And there is no cure.

Inside My Kid's Skin: Devotional

Blessed are the merciful,
for they shall receive mercy.

—Matthew 5:7 (NASB)

Over the years, I have spent hundreds of hours, hundreds of
dollars, and a lot of wear and tear on the car taking my sick
kids to a half a dozen counselors, therapists, psychologists,
and psychiatrists. We have had virtually no success in
getting the children to talk to us about their feelings
surrounding their illness or be fully compliant with their
prescribed treatments. Since they wouldn't open up to us,
we thought we'd give *the professionals* a try. But no.

A typical session would go like this:

Doctor: So how are you doing?

Child: Fine.

Doctor: I understand you have cystic fibrosis.

Child: Yup.

Doctor: So how do you feel about that?

Child: It sucks.

Doctor: I bet it does. So your mom tells me you don't do your treatments as you should.

Child: I do them sometimes, but not all of them.

Doctor: Why is that?

Child: I don't want to.

Doctor: Why not?

Child: It takes up too much time and doesn't do much good.

Doctor: Yeah, I can understand you feeling like that. It sounds like a drag.

That was pretty much the extent of their psychological treatment. McKenna went to a behavioral therapist for six or eight months but never learned to swallow pills, David never learned to spit out his mucus, and TJ was still dishonest with us (and probably himself) about his consistency in taking his enzymes.

Are the therapies, medications, and treatments for your child's illness difficult, painful, time-consuming, or scary? Do you wrestle with your child regarding compliance? It is exhausting, isn't it? It is important to have a good support system in place. Join a church, talk with friends, and strengthen your marriage. These are ways that have helped me cope when I've felt helpless.

> Thank You, Dear God,
> for understanding us and loving us.
> Our children are a mystery to us so often.
> I'm comforted by Your grace and mercy.
> Please comfort my child when I don't know how to.
> Thank You.
>
> Amen.

Heart Psalm 14
Dreams Have Changed

The lost dreams.

Dreams of the high-school football star.
Growing up.
Getting married, having children of his own.
Growing old.

Dreams are dashed on rocks
like waves on the shore.

Will my child grow up,
get married, have children?

I don't really know.
Does anyone?

What about the dreams the child has for himself?

He thinks,
Who would want to marry me?
That would be like buying a ticket
to board a sinking ship!

Why should I study in college?
I won't live long enough to have a career!

Dreams have had to change.

New dreams:
Graduating from high school.

…or…
Being happy today.
…ah…
Feeling secure in his eternity.

Dreams Have Changed: Devotional

> Hope deferred makes the heart sick,
> but a dream fulfilled is a tree of life.
>
> —Proverbs 13:12 (NLT)

A young couple has just given birth to their first child. You can spot them a mile away.

They have that spark in their eyes, their chests puff out a little, and their smiles are telling. Every subsequent child is just as special, but there is nothing like experiencing the first one.

We all live on that pink cloud, where we think our child could be the football star, the president of the United States, or Miss America.

When the diagnosis is made, we are shocked, devastated, and angry. Eventually, we grieve the loss of those dreams and must make new ones. We dust ourselves off, educate ourselves about something we never wanted to know about, and then get on with life—if we're lucky.

Some families don't survive intact. All that was bad in the couple's relationship is magnified under stress, but all that is good is also magnified *if* we choose to see the positive.

Do you struggle with the challenge of readjusting your ideals to your new reality? It's not a fun task but a necessary one if we are to live with the joy and abundance God promises. Our child's illness is not the end of the world; it's just the end of life as we knew it. Cling to God and to each other and hang on for dear life.

> Dear God,
>
> At such stressful times,
> please help us to cling to You
> and to each other.
> Help us to remember that
> You have plans for our children and our family.
> Maybe they are not what we had always dreamed of.
> But dreams have to change sometimes.
> Help me remember that Your plans for us
> are *beyond my wildest dreams*.
> Thank You.
>
> Amen.

Prayers, Notes, Reflections

Heart Psalm 15
It's Too Much

All the pills.
All the hours of daily treatments.
All the therapies.

It's Just Too Much!

"I don't want to do it all!"
my child says.

"Maybe it will buy me extra time,
maybe it won't,"
he reasons.

Extra time to do what?
More treatments?
he ponders.

Maybe it will help.
But maybe it is a waste of precious time and energy.

"I am not willing.

It is just too much.

And it's my decision."

It's Too Much: Devotional

Trust in the Lord with all your heart;
do not depend on your own understanding.
Seek his will in all you do, and he will show you
which path to take.

—Proverbs 3:5–6 (NLT)

Before one of his admittances, David and I had a talk with his doctor. The doctor listed all the things that were *mandatory* for good overall health maintenance. Previously, I had a homeopathic doctor come to see the kids, and she suggested many supplements. We purchased them, and the boys took them for several months, but they both decided it was too much to do. Since they couldn't feel any immediate benefit, they decided to discontinue the nonessentials.

So this doctor's list included a *minimum* of forty-seven pills and a *minimum* of four hours of respiratory therapy per day. The doctor asked David if he was willing to do all that. David answered honestly. "No, it's too much."

The truth is that even if David did all that, there would be no guarantee that it would all be successful. It might, but it might not. It could be a waste of precious time. It's a risky gamble.

What if he did all that stuff and then caught a bug that ravaged his lungs and killed him in a week? Or what if his lung suddenly started to bleed, and he drowned in his own blood in a matter of minutes? We've seen these things happen to others. Then all the maintenance he had previously done would have been a waste of time, time that he could have spent on activities of his own choosing.

Truth be told, as a newly diagnosed diabetic, my husband will only take the pill. He isn't willing to do the diet and daily blood monitoring, either. It is too much for some adults. It is way too much for most children. My husband can finally relate to the children's noncompliant attitude.

Do you ever feel overwhelmed? As overwhelmed as your child? Do you wonder what the right thing to do is? We have such a huge responsibility as the parent. Thank God He is *our* parent. He will guide us when we ask and listen.

> Dear God,
>
> How are we to know the right thing to do?
> My kids don't want to do all this stuff!
> I wouldn't either, if it was required of me.
> But they are just kids!
> Can't they just act like kids?
> Please, God?
> Please make it all worth it to them.
> Thank You.
>
> Amen.

Prayers, Notes, Reflections

_____

_____

_____

_____

_____

_____

_____

_____

_____

_____

_____

_____

_____

_____

_____

_____

_____

_____

_____

_____

_____

_____

_____

_____

_____

_____

Heart Psalm 16
Joy versus Grief

I didn't believe it.
Couldn't imagine it.
But it is true.

I have found that Unspeakable Joy
and Indescribable Grief
Can occupy the same space at the same time
under certain conditions.

When I live in the moment,
I can experience tremendous joy.

When I look to the future,
ask all the "what if" questions,
my grief chokes me.

I have learned to do both at the same time.

When I watch my child learning a new skill
or accomplishing a difficult task
or enjoying an activity,
my joy is full.
It overflows through my eyes.

Why can't I just leave it alone?
Why do I go "future hopping?"
Imagining the shortest timeline?
I could just kick myself!

But…no.
I must be patient with myself.
Tell myself to look at my child
and share his joy.

Live in this moment.

Breathe out the grief.
And breathe in joy.

Joy versus Grief: Devotional

Don't worry about anything; instead,
pray about everything.
Tell God what you need,
and thank him for all he has done.
Then you will experience God's peace,
which exceeds anything we can understand.

—Philippians 4:6–7 (NLT)

The first weekend we lived in Modesto, the Cystic Fibrosis Foundation (CFF) walkathon was held at Modesto Junior College. We were so busy moving that we hadn't gotten any sponsors ahead of time. But Tom's dad had been volunteering with CFF since his retirement from Ford at the time of David's diagnosis, so we thought we'd drop by.

As we arrived, David, TJ, and Jordan announced that they wanted to walk the course. It was five miles through the city streets along a mapped route. I was hesitant, but they insisted. I had long since given up the idea of trying to hold back the kids due to their illness, so we let them go.

I hung out at the end point of the route, where pizza and cold sodas waited for the victorious walkers. The first people to finish arrived, and then a few more. Different groups of people straggled in during the hot midday. We waited and watched and searched the crowd for our little boys.

Before long, the event organizers approached us and said, "We don't know where your little guys are. We want to drive the route to look for them." I wholeheartedly and gratefully agreed. What had I been thinking to let my sons loose in a new town with only a map? Did they even know how to read a map? At that time, David was not quite eleven, TJ was nine, and Jordan was about five years old.

I guess I thought they would just stick with the group. *But what about restrooms?* Two of the three boys have CF and can have sudden digestive distress. Were they okay? And it is such a hot day. I don't think they have any water. Will they get heat stroke and fry their brains? I was vexed with myself and worried for the boys.

After a very anxious few minutes, the search party returned—without the kids. They told me, "Well, we found them, but they refused a ride. They want to walk the rest of the way to the finish line."

I was so proud of them that day! They had kept themselves safe, read their maps, and finished triumphantly!

Are you filled with mixed and conflicting feelings about your child's accomplishments? It is hard to let them go. We want to hold on to them and keep them safe.

> Thank You, God, for the victories
> that bring joy in our lives.
> Sometimes they are the same experiences
> that bring grief.
> Please watch over our children.
> Keep them safe as they explore Your world.
> Thank You.
>
> Amen.

Heart Psalm 17
Please Understand

When a member of any family is sick…
…the whole family is sick.

We may become fragile.
We may feel frightened and confused.
We may need extra attention.

We may act out.
We don't mean to.
We just kind of fly apart, emotionally,
sometimes acting inappropriately.

Sometimes, we can't think straight.
We have a hard time concentrating.
We may strike out in anger…
…or out of fear.

Please try to understand…
…and be patient with us.

Thank you.

Please Understand: Devotional

> Now we who are strong
> ought to bear the weaknesses
> of those without strength
> and not just please ourselves.
>
> —Romans 15:1 (NASB)

The morning after I received the worst report from our child's doctor, I went to visit my grandmother. I knew I needed to tell her what the doctor had said, but I also needed her. She had always been in my life and was, in fact, my rock. I always relied on her and knew she was praying for me my whole life.

When I got to her apartment, she was preparing breakfast in her little kitchen. She is blind, so I went to her rather than waiting for her to come find me. As I began my story, she could hear the choke in my voice. Grandma opened her arms to me, and I fell into them as I continued my tale. We just stood there in her kitchen, hugging each other for about fifteen minutes, she listening to my grief and misery spilling out, not saying a word.

When I had emptied myself, Grandma prayed for me, my son, and our whole family. Her ninety years had taught her a lot about how to help others during challenging times. She didn't try to offer empty platitudes, quote scripture, or fancy sayings. She just stood with me, let me cry, and didn't try to offer a single word of comfort until I was through. And even then, she just spoke words to our loving Father, not to me. She just hugged and loved me. That was all the comfort I needed.

What great lessons the elderly hold for us. They are a treasure. I learn so much from my grandmother. I am blessed to have her in my life. Do you have a wise, elderly person in your life who you learn from? Your child can benefit greatly from such a relationship too. Expose your young person to the oldest generation. They are good for each other.

> Thank You, God, for placing each person in my life.
> The elderly are valuable,
> and the youngsters are refreshing.
> Together, we learn the lessons You lay before us.
> We are all gifts to each other.
> You are wise and generous!
> Thank You, again, for the gifts of my children
> and the elders in my life.
>
> Amen.

Prayers, Notes, Reflections

Heart Psalm 18
They Prick and Cut

My little child,
So beautiful and perfect.

His skin, so velvety soft.
His hair, so downy, so silky.

He is beautiful.
He is precious.
He is my child.

Then they cut his tender skin!
They prick him!
They shave his soft hair.
They operate.

They cut my child.
They slice
and add to
and remove
and stitch.

My child lives in agony
with the hope of getting well.
Will it all be worth it?
Will it buy us time?
Enough time?

They Prick and Cut: Devotional

Hear my prayer, O Lord!
And let my cry for help come to Thee.
Do not hide Thy face from me
in the day of my distress:
Incline Thine ear to me: In the day when I call
answer me quickly.

—Psalm 102:1–2 (NASB)

It is inconceivable. Unimaginable. Unbelievable.

How can any human being alive on the face of the earth possibly puncture the skin of our perfect baby with needle or scalpel? Cause our child to cry and suffer?

They do it to save life or limb or as a part of a necessary procedure.

It is hard for me to see past my immediate situation. Perhaps I should pray for each member of our medical team each day. Perhaps it wears on them to cause pain to children every day. I know *I* wouldn't like to do it. I would have to harden my heart to the screams and cries of the little ones. Maybe that is what they do. But how do they turn their feelings back on when they go home?

Do you struggle with feelings toward your child's medical staff? Are you sometimes angry at them for seeming apathetic toward your child's suffering? For *causing* your child's suffering? I guess I feel as my child does about his medication. We know it is curative, but it feels like a curse. Our medical team has to do certain things that injure our soul because it hurts our child. In the end, though, it is for our child's own good. Let us support them in every way we can. Let us show our gratitude for their caring and expertise with our child.

Dear Lord,

Please comfort our children as they endure all the medical procedures.
Please be with us, the parents, who suffer along with our children.
And, Lord, please be with each member of our health-care team.
Show them love—perhaps through me.
Help them do their job well and skillfully as they care for my child.
And also, strengthen their relationships at home and bring them joy.
Thank You, precious Lord.

Amen.

Our Story:
And Still More

Well, wouldn't you know it? When McKenna was six months old, I joyfully found myself pregnant again. It sure wasn't easy taking care of four children, three who were health challenged, while morning sickness ran rampant. But somehow, we made it through again.

Baby number 5 was the only baby to be born on his due date, which was July 25, 1994. I had a prenatal appointment on that day, and I was beginning to dilate, so the doctor admitted me for delivery.

Jordan was born later that evening at a healthy ten pounds, eight ounces. His entrance was pretty dramatic. His umbilical cord was wrapped around his neck. The delivery staff had to slant the bed, so my head tipped down, and my feet tilted way up in the air. It was extremely difficult to push the baby out against gravity.

When Jordan finally made his appearance, he was blue and in a bit of distress. His medical condition improved immediately, but his face was speckled with little hemorrhages due to the speed of his delivery.

Before we took Jordan home, a doctor came into my hospital room, took Jordan in his arms, and rubbed a tiny bottlebrush on the inside of his mouth to collect some skin cells. It was a new way of doing the test for cystic fibrosis without having to take blood. However, he rubbed Jordan's cheek so hard and long that Jordan's mouth was bleeding, and he was screaming when the doctor gave him back to me.

A week later, we got Jordan's genetic test back. He had inherited only one copy of the cystic fibrosis gene, making him a nonsymptomatic *carrier* of the defective gene. He did not have cystic fibrosis. We were relieved, but we did not celebrate. We had to be fine with whatever way the results came out, so we didn't have our hearts set one way or the other. Things would be a lot less work this way. That is all.

Predictably, I learned of my next pregnancy before Jordan was a year old. This pregnancy was a bit more miserable toward the end because I developed gestational diabetes. I learned to do something I never dreamed I could do: give myself injections.

You would think that after doing four finger pokes a day and injecting my enormous belly with insulin two times per day, it would get easier, even become *old hat* after a while. Not so. I never got used to it. I felt faint and had to rally my courage every time.

I followed the diet religiously and adhered to my treatments because the life and health of the baby depended on it. It was so hard. I don't know if I would have been willing to do it if it was to benefit just me. But it was explained to me that the baby could develop the opposite of diabetes, hypoglycemia, if I didn't take care of myself. It was good motivation.

The worst effect diabetes had on me was debilitating exhaustion. I could do only one major chore a day. I had to choose between showering *or* cooking dinner *or* doing a load of laundry.

Poor Tom. Every day he came home from a hard day of work and shopped for groceries, cooked dinner for everyone, took a shower, threw a load of laundry into the washer, and fell into bed. I don't know who welcomed the conclusion of that pregnancy more, me or him.

The day my water broke was one of the happiest days of our lives because the diabetes would likely disappear when the baby was born. When we checked into the hospital, Tom began boasting to the nurses about how this was our sixth baby and how he could probably deliver it himself.

The attending doctor looked about fifteen years old. She had been listening to Tom's bragging for a couple of hours. When we went to the delivery room, she slapped a pair of latex gloves on him.

"Step up to the plate."

Tom's were the first hands to touch Shannon, born on March 3, 1996. She was no lightweight either, weighing in at ten pounds, three ounces. And she had a skeptical, grumpy look on her face that we couldn't coax away for over three months. Before leaving the hospital, Shannon gave a DNA sample to test for CF.

While recovering from delivery and the gestational diabetes, my exhaustion continued for a week and a half.

This was inconvenient because when Shannon was four days old, she developed a fever of over 102, a worrisome temperature in newborns. Since I was still too weak to stand or walk while holding the baby, it was impossible for me to take her to the emergency room.

So I stayed home with the other children while Tom ran Shannon to the hospital. I thought they would just check her out and tell us to give her Tylenol or something, but Tom called to tell me they had admitted Shannon to the NICU and wanted to do a spinal tap to check for meningitis.

I totally freaked! I had just had an epidural four days earlier during Shannon's birth, which was similar to the procedure they wanted to perform on my newborn, so I knew it was going to be a horrible experience for the baby. I told Tom not to let them do the procedure until I got there.

Tom drove home, and I drove back to the hospital to spend the next several days with Shannon. They took her to the procedure room down the hall and did the spinal tap while I waited in her room and cried for her. When they brought her back to me, they had to insert an IV to administer antibiotics just in case her test came back positive. It didn't. Thank God.

While we were in the hospital taking care of Shannon's fever issue, her pediatrician got a message to me that her CF test came back. It was negative. But she was a carrier, like Jordan. When Shannon recovered, we went home, once again, to begin our new lives as a family of eight.

J O R D A N

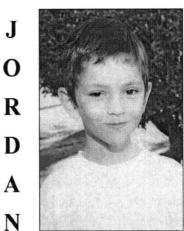

S
H
A
N
N
O
N

4

EIGHT IS ENOUGH

Heart Psalm 19
Life on Hold

It is entirely possible that

Doctors
Technicians
Transcribers
Nurses
Diagnosticians
File clerks
typists
And whoever else falls in the line of protocol
to handle information regarding
our children's test results,
may never have waited, themselves,
to receive a test result for their own child.

Don't they know that every minute feels like a day?
Every day feels like a year?
Can they not imagine that we are waiting
with bated breath?
That every moment that our child's
potential condition goes untreated,
it is likely worsening?
Don't they realize that the problem is growing?

It is just words on paper to them.
The paper passes through their hands
with no consequence.

Just one more family that will receive
life-altering news.
What do they care?

It is our child's very life.

Until we get the call with the information,
we cannot breathe, make plans, function, live.

Our life is on hold.

Life on Hold: Devotional

But the fruit of the Spirit is love, joy, peace, patience,
kindness, goodness, faithfulness, gentleness, self-
control; against such things there is no law.

—Galatians 5:22–23 (NASB)

My four-year-old was in the hospital being tested for diabetes. He also had cystic fibrosis. His white blood cell count was up because of a lung infection. That was nothing new. It was the test results for the diabetes that I was interested in finding out. They said the results would be ready in the morning.

What time in the morning?

Morning, to me, means 5:00 a.m., but I would be patient. I would wait until the beginning of the workday, 9:00 a.m., before I started bugging the staff for any news. At 8:59 a.m., I was ready to pounce. There is a nurse.

"Have you heard anything.?"

"You'll need to talk with the doctor."

"Where is he?"

"With another patient."

Aargh! Okay, I'll wait my turn, but I'm sure the other patient's needs aren't as important as mine and my kid's.

I wait.

There he is!

"Doctor, Doctor, do you have the result of my child's test?"

"Yes, come here with me." We walk down the hall to a light board. "See here? His chest X-rays show some clouding but no pneumonia. This is good news."

A nurse interrupts. The doctor is needed elsewhere.

"Excuse me," he says as he walks away.

What? Wait a minute! You didn't tell me what I wanted to know! What about the diabetes? Aaarggghhh! How clueless can a person be? How could he *not* know that I needed to know the *other* test results?

Another time, my fifteen-year-old was being tested for thyroid cancer. "Your doctor will contact you next week," said the technician at the conclusion of the test.

Next week! How could I wait until *next week*? If there was news to know, I wanted to know it *now*. I called the radiology department, repeatedly, to see if there were reports recorded in the computerized file.

"Yes, there are."

"Well, read them to me, please!" I said.

"Something was found. She needs more tests. Someone will contact you in a few days to schedule the follow-up appointment."

A few days? In a few days, *if she has cancer*, cells could have broken off and started growing in other places of my child's body! A few days are a lifetime! No, "a few days" isn't good enough! I want action—now!

I feel a lesson coming on.

Patience, kindness, compassion—these are hard virtues to live when we are in stressful situations, but that is when they are most needed.

Dear Lord,

Please grant me patience,
and I want it *now*!
Oops, sorry. That's not the way it works. Rats!
Okay, dear Lord,
thank You for the situations You put me in
that cause me to exercise patience. Please help me!
Thank You.

Amen.

Heart Psalm 20
Milestones

Smiling, rolling over, walking, talking.
First day of school, birthdays, driving.
Going on the first date, graduations.
Moving out, going away to college.
Getting a job, getting married.
Purchasing a house, having children.

The "firsts" and the "biggies."
They are meaningful to all families.

But to us, we are ever aware
that the future is so uncertain.

Our child may not have time
to live, to reach,
to pass the milestones
that others take in stride.

We grasp tightly to the moment,
the event, the activity
and try to feel it more deeply.
Try to remember it more clearly.
We take more pictures and videos.
Because…we know.
There may not be a next time.
A next year. A tomorrow.

Another Milestone.

Our child's additional Milestone list:
Learning to swallow pills
The first hospitalization
The first IV
Getting a G tube surgically implanted in his stomach
The first PICC line
The first portacath placement
The first lung bleed
The first endoscopy
The first self-administered insulin injection

And, of course, the ultimate milestone yet to come...
...death.

Milestones: Devotional

There is an appointed time for everything.
And there is a time for every event under heaven—
A time to give birth, and a time to die;

—Ecclesiastes 3:1–2 (NASB)

"So shall I tell the nurse to call over to the ward and reserve a bed for you?"

"Yeah."

An hour later, we drove from the clinic parking garage two blocks away to the hospital garage. After a brief stop in the admitting office and a ride up the elevator, David was resting in his bed in a private room on the tenth-floor pediatric ward. It will be his last stay on this ward, as he will no longer be a pediatric patient after this hospitalization. David's eighteenth birthday was just over a month away.

After eating my lunch, I was in David's bathroom brushing my teeth as it occurred to me that David, who lives in a house with nine other people, now had what he'd desired when he became a legal adult: his own apartment.

I called out to him, "Hey, David, you have your own room and your own bathroom. Cute nurses come to take care of you. Someone from dietary brings you food. Respiratory therapists come to do your treatments for you, and housekeeping takes away the garbage and cleans up. You have moved out! This is your bachelor pad!"

Exhausted, nauseous, and miserable, David was curled up on his hospital gurney. As he lay there trying to rest, without even opening his eyes, he uttered weakly, "I'm not laughing, Mom."

In all honesty, neither was I.

The progression of our child's disease, the day-to-day caring for an ill loved one is emotionally draining. We want them to experience a normal life with all it brings. But it is not to be. We have to ask God to help us adjust our expectations and to help us as we approach the uncertain times.

Dear God,

You know that children should not die
before their parents,
and yet You completely understand our plight.
You had a Son who also died. He suffered terribly.
You must have also suffered as You watched.
Thank You for comforting us
as we walk a similar road.

Amen.

Heart Psalm 21
Normal Family

I wonder what it would be like
to be a
Normal Family

For Normal Families,
the most pressing issues
in the children's lives are

Getting good grades
Studying for next week's math test
Making the soccer team
Auditioning for the school play
Or getting the cute kid in English class
to notice them.

For their parents, I imagine it is

Getting the job promotion
Planning the next vacation
Keeping up with the Joneses

Because we are not a
Normal Family,
our most pressing issues are

Waiting for results from the latest
Scan
Blood test

X-ray
Lung, heart, liver, kidney function test
MRI
Psychiatric, academic, neurologic evaluation

And figuring out how to pay the mounting medical
and pharmaceutical bills.
Dealing with the "well" kids as well as the "sick" kids.
Wondering how much longer our sick kid will live
and how much he will suffer before being released
from this life.
And how we will live without him.

And on and on.

I wonder what it would be like to be a Normal Family.

Normal Family: Devotional

Behold, children are a gift of the Lord.
How blessed is the man whose quiver is full of them.

—Psalm 127:3,5 (NASB)

Is there such thing as a normal family? I used to think a
family down the block was the perfect family, but I was
assured that everyone has their secrets and flaws. There is
no such thing as a perfect family.

But a normal family?

If we didn't have an inherited disease, we would still be a *large* family. But we didn't always have eight children. We got them one at a time. But *normal?* What would be different about us?

I know one thing. I probably wouldn't have let my kids run in the house or jump on the beds. But because of their disease, I never wanted to limit their physical activity. Running and jumping is good for them, so we extended the loosened rules for all our children.

Oh, another thing, I would never have been so free with the snack foods or so lax with meal arrangements, but our sick kids need to eat as many calorie-rich foods as possible, so I made many, many concessions. And I didn't always want to limit the fun food to the sick kids, or else the others would be even more resentful than they already were.

I know there would have been other differences too. It's just hard to picture how it would have been. But in all honesty, it doesn't really matter. Because we must deal in *what is*, not in *what could have been*. We are not a normal family and never will be, but we are the family God made us into. And He had a really good reason for it.

Our family is *unique*, and so is yours. Maybe we *are* a normal family, normal for *us*. But we will never be *average*, no matter how you slice it.

> Thank You, God, for making our family the way it is.
> Each person is vital and necessary
> and teaches the rest of us lessons

that only they can, by Your design.
Please help us to love and appreciate one another
the way You do.
Thank You.

Amen.

Heart Psalm 22
We Are More Than the Disease

Thank you for asking how my sick child is doing.

But please remember…

Our family is more than The Disease.

We have other children.
We have interests, hobbies, and activities.
We have other concerns, troubles, and struggles
besides The Disease.
We like to talk about subjects other than medical "stuff."
Sometimes, we need a break from it.

We want to know how you
and your family are doing, too.

So…how are *you*?

My child wants you to know
that he is more than The Disease.

My child wants you to know
that he is a *person*,
not just a *patient*.

He has interests, opinions, talents, joys, and pain.

My child wants you to see more than the IV pole,
the needles and machines and bottles of pills.

My child wants you to hear more
than the hacking cough.
My child doesn't want you to see
the goo that he coughs up
or the body that is wasting away
or becoming deformed from The Disease.
My child doesn't want you to smell the odors
that come from The Disease.

My child has a message for you:

I AM MORE THAN MY DISEASE!
PLEASE LOOK CLOSER AND SEE ME
FOR WHO I AM!

We Are More Than the Disease: Devotional

Rejoice with those who rejoice,
and weep with those who weep.

—Romans 12:15 (NASB)

Childhood diseases—or their treatments—cause many beautiful children to lose their hair, become unrecognizably bloated, hunch-shouldered, and barrel-chested from coughing, and their spines become crooked. Some illnesses make them blind; some become skeletally thin.

They may lose limbs or develop skin sores. They have multiple scars from surgeries and procedures. Their joints become swollen and painful. They become confined to wheelchairs, tethered to oxygen tanks and feeding tube pumps.

It is heartbreaking to see our beautiful, active children lose themselves as they waste away.

Are our kids still themselves even when they look different and lose their mobility, their consciousness, their minds, their lives?

Yes…and no.

Much of who we are to others and to ourselves is wrapped up in what we look like. When our child's appearance changes with illness, their self-perception changes.

Yet, their essence is still in there, inside the shell, the tent, the bodies that house their spirit.

How are we to respond to their changing bodies?

Since we know them intimately and love them desperately, it is easy for us to overlook or ignore the subtle daily changes. It is not so easy for the casual friend or neighbor who drops by only occasionally.

How can we help the visitor feel at ease during the awkward visits? How can we help them remember that our child is more than his or her disease?

> Dear Lord, teach us how to be a
> loving friend and neighbor.
> Remind us why You gave us two ears
> and only one mouth.
> Keep us all in Your loving care.
> Thank You, dear Lord.
>
> Amen.

Prayers, Notes, Reflections

Heart Psalm 23
Time Bomb

She coughed and choked all night long.
She woke to a terrifying, gruesome discovery:
Blood on her mouth, her hand, her pillow.

During the night,
unbeknownst to her,
her lung bled.
She choked on the blood, and it caused her to cough,
splattering it about.

Thankfully, the bleed sealed itself.

But what if it hadn't?
What if it happens again?

When?
Will it stop?

Or will she bleed to death while I sleep?

I lay awake and listen to her cough.
She is a time bomb.

Tick, tick, tick, tick, tick, tick, tick, tick, tick, tick,
tick, tick, tick...

Time Bomb: Devotional

For we are God's masterpiece.
He has created us anew in Christ Jesus,
so we can do the good things
He planned for us long ago.

—Ephesians 2:10 (NLT)

Sometimes, our sick daughter's condition makes her so fragile we don't even want to breathe around her, afraid she will blow away like gold leaf. If we touch her, she will dissolve into nothingness like cotton candy on our tongue, leaving only a hint of sweetness. Hug her, hold her tight? No, never! We might hurt her, break her, crush her.

But how can we not?

I can't help but wonder what I will think about when her life is over. Will she ever have existed? Will we remember her? Will she be mere figments of our imagination, hiding in the corners of our consciousness? A memory of someone we once knew, just a picture hanging on the wall?

After living through a close call, it is difficult to get back to "normal," where our nerves are not always close to the surface, where the stress level can go back down to a low simmer, where breathing becomes automatic again, not a conscious effort.

But after a while, it is possible. Until next time.

Does your child's illness cause her to have crisis situations that set your nerves on edge? How do you manage the stress it causes? Does it get easier with time? Have you turned over the results of each crisis event to God, trusting that He will hold you tight if your child dies? Each event is an opportunity to exercise your faith muscles.

> Dear Lord,
>
> You gave us our precious child to love and care for. We don't understand why it has to be so difficult sometimes.
> We don't know why You allow certain things.
> Please help us to trust You and Your plan.
> And please also comfort us and our child when things get intense.
> Thank You.
>
> Amen.

Prayers, Notes, Reflections

Heart Psalm 24
No Do-Overs

Am I a good parent?
Am I doing things right?
Will my children turn out okay?

Have I taught my sick child
the best way to care for himself?

I know our families disapprove of our methods.
Our child's doctors have scorned our way of life…
"You have too many children!"
"You should make them do this and that
and thus and such!"
"More treatments! Less fun!"

We have chosen to live life.
We choose more fun and a less rigid way of life.

I know! I know!
My sick child will not live as long
as he possibly could have!
I know! I know!!
I torture myself with that knowledge!

But there are no do-overs.
No second chances.
Only second-guessing.

But…

We have a good relationship with our child.
He is at peace with his life.
He accepts the hand he has been dealt.
He loves God and has found purpose.

Is there more we could have done?

NO!

We have done well.

If we could,
 we would not
do anything different.

Well...maybe...

No Do-Overs: Devotional

Just as a father has compassion on *his* children,
So the Lord has compassion on those who fear Him.

—Psalm 103:13 (NASB)

Over the years, my husband and I have differed in our philosophies about many things. For most of them, we can agree to disagree, but on the issue of our children's health, we have to agree on most things, especially when dealing with medical decisions. We can't give the medical staff two different definitive answers to their pressing questions.

One big difference has to do with the children's home care. We have been taught that our job, as parents, is to work our way out of our job. We are supposed to train and teach our children to be self-sufficient, so by the time they are legal adults, they won't need Mom or Dad to support them or care for their household needs, like laundry and cooking. If they don't want to care for themselves, let them suffer the consequences. This is a gradual process and doesn't happen the day before their eighteenth birthday.

What does this mean for our sick kids? All along, we are to teach them to do inventory of their medications so they can phone the pharmacy to order refills. They are to learn to do their therapies at the right time without Mom or Dad reminding them. They should learn to take care of their diet and exercise, as well as take their prescribed medications properly.

What if they don't do the necessary medical care, not to mention the regular stuff, like laundry and homework? The consequences can be dire. Do we continuously bail them out? How will they learn if we keep catching them before they hit the ground?

Here's an even greater issue that we have had differing opinions about: What if your sick kid says he has had enough? He is sick and tired of being sick and tired. He doesn't want to do it anymore. All the therapies and medications don't help him get better; they just slow down the rate of decline. He is through. Just leave him alone.

Wow. This is hard to hear. It is hard to imagine a young person feeling so miserable for so many years that he loses his will to live. I have always been extremely healthy, so I can't begin to imagine how he feels.

Well, my husband got mad and wanted to yell some sense into our child. As the mother, I wanted to respect our child's feelings and let him make his own decision. He had just turned eighteen, so he could really do as he pleased.

Thank God he started to feel better and he found enough good things in his life to look forward to, so he began to do the minimum health care to restore a measure of wellness to his life. He began to participate in activities that were meaningful to him, and he has miraculously survived these several more years.

If your child is at the end of her strength, ask God to revive her and lift her spirit. Or to help you to let go.

> Dear Lord, even as we surrender our child to You,
> we thank You for the extra time
> You have granted our child.
> It seems that regardless of the decisions we make,
> Your plan still prevails.
> Even so, Lord, please guide us
> and strengthen our relationship
> with each other and with our child.
> Thank You.
>
> Amen.

Our Story:
A Delightful Quiver!

Before long, another pregnancy test came back positive, and again, I was miserably sick. I was admitted to the hospital for IV fluids to treat my dehydration resulting from vomiting, just as I had with three of the previous pregnancies.

I was thankful when the morning sickness subsided. I felt terrific for my remaining months. I managed to control my blood sugars with diet during this pregnancy, and as my time drew close, I was grateful that I didn't develop diabetes this time.

I was scheduled for a doctor's visit just one week into my ninth month. During the cervix check, my doctor exclaimed, "Oh, my!"

"What's going on?" I asked.

She said, "You're in labor! You are dilated to five and need to get admitted to the hospital immediately!"

I checked into the hospital at about seven that evening, but the baby took her sweet time. She didn't make her appearance until 2:20 the following afternoon.

Lynnsey was three weeks early, but she weighed eight pounds even. Well, actually, her birth record says she weighed seven pounds, fifteen ounces, but as she was carried from my body across the room to the scale, she peed the whole way, so I figure she lost at least an ounce en route.

Some time before leaving the hospital, she also generously gave a DNA sample to be tested for CF.

On Lynnsey's way out of the hospital, we were told to take her to the clinic the next day for a bilirubin count, as she was quite jaundiced. As it turned out, she needed to go back into the hospital for a day or two for phototherapy. She needed to lie with only a diaper on under special lights to help remove the toxins from her body until her kidneys kicked in.

While we were in the hospital, Lynnsey's CF test results came back. She was negative on both sides. She was our only child, we would later discover, who wasn't even a carrier of the defective CF gene.

Our lives revolved around church, school, and, of course, doctor appointments and breathing treatments. We tried to live as normally as possible and give the children happy childhoods.

Tom and I attended my twenty-year high-school reunion the following summer. That very night, after the reunion, I got pregnant again.

By this time, Tom and I didn't have the heart to make another unwelcome pregnancy announcement to our families, so we decided to not tell them. We would just wait until I started to show, and they could guess or ask us, but it became a moot point as twelve weeks later, I miscarried.

It helped my healing process a lot, I think, to be pregnant again by the time the lost baby's due date rolled around.

As Tom and I were eating breakfast at a medical conference in the late summer of 2000, we had a life-altering conversation. I told him, "I think God is telling me that we should not have any more children after this one is born. What do you think?"

He emphatically agreed. We decided to call his doctor after the baby was born and schedule a vasectomy.

My midwife and I decided to induce the baby's birth if I hadn't had her by November 10. The date came and went, so I was admitted into the hospital in Modesto after the weekend on Monday morning, November 13, 2000. I was examined, an IV was inserted into the back of my left hand, my preferred and well-used site, and we set in to wait.

It didn't take long. When I was dilated to five, I went to use the bathroom. When I came out, I was checked again and was found to be dilated to eight. My midwife turned up my Pitocin, and I became very uncomfortable. In a matter of thirty minutes, she said, "You're fully dilated. Do you feel like pushing?"

"Not really, but I'll give it a try."

I was lying on my left side, and someone had given me a cool washcloth for my forehead. With my next contraction, I covered my eyes with the washcloth and pushed as if my life depended on it. When the contraction was over, I had a new daughter.

Nina weighed nine pounds, twelve ounces and had a full head of soft brown hair. Delivering the placenta wasn't any fun, but when that task was completed, I felt so unbelievably terrific, I could have jumped up and turned cartwheels! It was an extraordinary delivery and a fantastic ending to my birthing career.

A week later, we were notified that Nina's CF test was concluded. It indicated that she inherited one copy of the CF gene. Nina is a carrier.

Two months after Nina was born, Kelsey was sick. As she was having her blood drawn for testing, I suggested that they take an extra vial and do her genotype for CF carrier status, since, technically, at age 14, she was of child-bearing age. (The medical staff had found no reason to have the expensive test done until she became old enough to potentially have children.) So the sample was taken and sent off to the lab. A week or two later, we found out that Kelsey is also a carrier of the defective CF gene.

What that means for Kelsey, as well as our other kids who carry the CF gene, is that whenever she decides to get married or there is opportunity of getting pregnant, she should have her partner genotyped also, so they will know if he is a carrier or not. If her partner is a carrier also, they would have a 25 percent chance of having a baby with CF and a 50 percent chance that the baby would be a nonsymptomatic carrier of the CF gene. The baby would have a 25 percent chance of neither having CF or of being a carrier, like Lynnsey.

If her partner was *not* a carrier, their baby would have a 25 percent chance of being a carrier and a 75 percent chance of not being a carrier. The baby would definitely not have CF.

Of course, if her partner *had* CF, the chances of having a baby (which would be slim, anyway) with CF increase to 75 percent, and the other 25 percent would definitely produce a baby who was a carrier.

Being tested enables them to make an informed decision whether to risk having a baby with CF or if they should choose to look into adoption instead.

So our final tally is three children (David, TJ, and McKenna) with cystic fibrosis, four (Kelsey, Jordan, Shannon, and Nina) are carriers, and one child (Lynnsey) who is not a carrier.

L
Y
N
N
S
E
Y

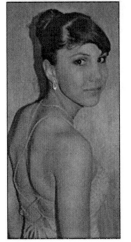

Nina

5

REALITY BITES. BITE BACK!

Heart Psalm 25
Bucket List

How many kids do you know
who have a
bucket list?

How absurd!

But how many kids do you know
who know that they will die
before they grow up?

So these kids think of what they want to do
or learn
or accomplish
before they get too sick
to do anything
…before they kick the bucket.

Go to Disneyland
See a 3-D or IMAX movie
Ride in an airplane
Meet their favorite movie star or pop singer
Write a book
Learn to play an instrument
Sing before an audience
Climb a mountain
Visit a foreign country
Learn to ride a bike or drive a car
Experience their first kiss

As their parents…
our greatest wish
besides *the* cure,
is to aid our child
in accomplishing their

bucket list

no matter what the cost or sacrifice.

What else can we do for them?

Bucket List: Devotional

We can make our own plans,
but the Lord gives the right answer.

—Proverbs 16:1(NLT)

A year before David turned eighteen and graduated from high school, he expressed a strong desire to move out when he became of legal age. Tom and I experienced great trepidation regarding this plan. After all, he wouldn't even take care of himself while we were near, watching and reminding. What would happen if he was free from parental supervision?

But we had to consider, *Should we try to prevent him from moving out?* Of course not. Legally, he is able to move out if he wants to. *Should we help him?* Absolutely. *What happens if he gets sick?* He will either die or call the doctor and go in the hospital. *Can we live with the consequences?* What choice do we have?

I had to realize a couple of things. David may be thinking about all the rights of passage that most kids go through—graduation, driving, college, living away from home, marriage, sex, career, children.

For some reason, David has been reluctant to learn to drive. And considering his health and expected lifespan, I don't think *David thinks* he could find anyone who would want to marry him. And since we have taught our children that sex is to be reserved for marriage, perhaps David thinks he will never experience *that* all-important rite of passage either. I have even taught our children that the first kiss should be at the marriage altar to ensure their purity is preserved *in its entirety* as a gift for their future spouse, so the first kiss may be out, too.

David's disease will most likely prevent him from fathering children naturally, which is a tragedy considering how much he loves babies. Adoption could be an option, but an expensive one. He is too exhausted to consider college or a career. So all that is left is high school graduation and living on his own. That doesn't leave much to look forward to.

So will I help him find a place to live? You bet I will!

Is your child making decisions that may greatly affect his life? Now would be the perfect time to commit him back to the Lord.

Dear God,

I trust that you are working behind the scenes,
working out the details.
You know the perfect situation for my child
to move into.
Just please don't take him very far away.
Thank You.

Amen.

Heart Psalm 26
The Thief

No! Not again!! Not this time!!! Please?!

How does *It* know
exactly when our moments of joy
should be interrupted and ruined?

My child tries to live normally,
enjoying an accomplishment
or a joke
or playing games with friends.

Our child is enjoying life.
He is happy.
I am so happy to see *him* happy
and *laughing.*

It lays in waiting
for the perfect moment to strike.

The time is right,
and *It* hits,
robbing us of the perfect moment.

It appears suddenly.
It jars us out of the moment.
It steals our peace and joy.
It causes breathlessness, headaches, and pain.
It chokes my child until he vomits.

It is explosive…

…The Damn Cough!
Brought on by the excess mucus
produced by the disease
and aroused by my child's laughter.

I AM ANGRY!

My child can't even laugh like other kids.
It stole away our perfect moment of joy.

I want to choke *It*
like *It* chokes my child!

The Thief: Devotional

Let everything that has breath,
Praise the Lord!

—Psalm 150:6 (NASB)

As we were planning for TJ's fourth birthday, he told us he wanted a juggling clown at his party. Well, we couldn't afford a clown. *Where do you find a clown?*

At this juncture in our lives, we learned that saying, "Maybe we can afford it next year," didn't cut it. No one, especially families directly affected by progressive, chronic illness, has any guarantees that *next year* will come.

But neither were we inclined to go into debt to afford some of the luxuries that would make life more fun. We had traveled down that road before and didn't want to repeat the mistake. So Tom put on one of my old formal dresses, and we painted up his face with my lipstick and makeup, and he was TJ's "clown." And he juggled, too!

We purchased a bike with training wheels for TJ's gift, but when his big party day arrived, he was sick. We had the party anyway, but he spent most of the time lying on the couch. When we gave him the bike, he smiled, said, "Thank you," rode it across the front of the house once, and then went back in the house to lie back down.

The next day, David, TJ, and McKenna all had fevers and bad coughs. Their breathing sounded terrible, very labored. As they all slept on the couch, feverish, and hacking occasionally, I sat nearby, overwhelmed, and I thought, *They are all going to die. They can hardly breathe.* It was a dark, dark day. I felt I would suffocate on the hopelessness, fear, and guilt. I could barely function.

Days that are supposed to be especially happy are especially hard when our child is sick. How can we begin to cope with the illness *and* everyday life? By praising God even when it seems ridiculous. We are in crisis and still should praise God? That's the perfect time! Begin with a gratitude list. What are you thankful for? I have to write my list while my children are well so I can remind myself when I am not thinking clearly when they are ill.

Dear Lord, it is especially hard to remember
to be joyful
and to praise You when I am in the depths of crisis
and my kids are in agony.
It feels very unfair to have illness taint an occasion
that is supposed to be only happy,
like a birthday celebration.
Please remind me that You are always here,
loving and caring about me and my kids.
Thank You.

Amen

Heart Psalm 27
Back Burner

Grief is always simmering away on the back burner.

Sometimes, it is turned up, and it bubbles,
nearly boiling over.
Requiring more attention,
we move it to the front burner.

But then…

We manage the crisis…or not.
Things take a turn for the better…this time.
The emergency is over…for now.
We live through another exacerbation…somehow.

And then it is turned down, and it calms.
We move the pot to the back burner again
and forget about it…nearly.

We go on with life.
Act as if we are a normal family
who does not have to think of such tragic things.

Like illness.
Like suffering.
Like death.

And how to go on.

I am curious to know what it would be like
not to have a pot simmering
on the back burner.

But I will never know.

I resent the pot.

Back Burner: Devotional

Yet you do not know what your life
will be like tomorrow.
You are just a vapor that appears for a little while
and then vanishes away.

—James 4:14 (NASB)

When the children all got sick, I started thinking, obsessively, about their funerals. I would make lists of songs I'd heard in church that I thought would be appropriate to comfort the mourners. I mentally picked out pictures for slide presentations that would be suitable for sharing with the congregation, that would show the wonderfulness of each child.

I think it was my way of protecting myself from being emotionally broadsided again. I thought that if I accepted the inevitability of the kids' death little by little, it would be easier when it finally happened.

That is the other thing about chronic, life-shortening illness. The reality of the eventuality of the final health decline always simmers on the back burner of my mind. It's not a fatalistic thought, but it is always just there. I feel as if I can never be 100 percent carefree because that pot is always simmering, waiting to heat up and boil over. I learned, many years later, that there is a psychological term for this phenomenon.

It is called constant grief.

There are no guarantees in life. There are only choices. Like Abraham Lincoln said, "Most folks are about as happy as they make up their minds to be." He suffered many hardships too, so I think he knew what he was talking about. It is a discipline that takes practice.

When you find that your mind is full of chaos, stop, take a deep breath, and offer a prayer of thanksgiving. It may take a moment or two to think of a blessing to be thankful for, but it becomes easier with practice.

> Only You, Lord, know what is to come.
> Only You know how much time each of us has.
> You knew it, ordained it,
> before You created the universe.
> Please help me trust that You know best.
> Especially when things don't make sense to me
> or I don't like what is happening,
> please remind me that You are God
> and have a purpose for everything.

I don't have to understand or like it.
Just accept it.
Boy, it's hard!
Please help me!
Thank You.

Amen.

Heart Psalm 28
Question 6

We don't say the word *sucks* at our house.
But it really describes this much better
than the word *stinks*.

My fourteen-year-old brought home an assignment
that had already been turned in and graded.
I could tell by reading it
that it was a beginning-of-the-year assignment,
answering questions
that had been asked
so the students could get to know each other.

I could figure out what the audible questions were
by the answers my child wrote.
Such as:

A. Funny, active, caring, fun.
The question must have been:
Q. Use four words to describe yourself.

And then:
A. animals, House MD, music
The question was:
Q. List three things you enjoy.

Here is the part that sucks:
A. spiders, dying, growing up.

Question six was:
Q. List three things you are afraid of.

Perhaps other children answered "dying" too.
But my child's fear is valid and tangible.
And, to her, growing up means dying.
Her fear is so real, she can taste it.

I didn't know she thought about that.
She shouldn't *have* to worry about that.

I can relate, but not exactly.
I know I will die.
But I didn't think about it happening
all through my childhood
like she does.

That really sucks.

Question 6: Devotional

For God has not given us a spirit of fear and timidity,
but of power, love,
and self discipline.

—2 Timothy 1:7 (NLT)

Childhood.

I envision beautiful bassinets with pastel-colored ribbons and bows, music boxes playing lullabies, adoring relatives singing and cooing to the infant, the carefree toddler laughing while swinging to and fro at the park, the happy preschooler at dance class and art lessons, building sand castles at the beach, the indecisive preteen trying on earrings at the mall, the confident high schooler chatting with friends on the phone, playing sports at school.

A nice picture.

What doesn't belong is the child's day being interrupted and disturbed by thoughts of death and dying, experiencing the momentary terror until she can push the thought back to the quiet recesses of her mind, until next time.

It is unfair. The piece doesn't fit in the picture!

But perhaps those thoughts cause her to think of God, to draw nearer to Him, nearer than other kids ever do. Do you think it is an even trade?

Maybe we can use a school paper with question 6 to open dialogue with our children. It can be an opportunity to discover hidden feelings and beliefs that otherwise would not have been revealed.

Discovering more about our children's thoughts and feelings is such a gift! It is sometimes painful but always a valuable treasure.

> Dear Lord,
>
> I am not qualified to decide what is good or bad,
> what is right or wrong, what is just or unjust.
> I am not Your judge.
> That would be beyond presumptuous.

Please teach me to trust You, no matter what.
Thank You, most gracious Lord,

Amen.

Heart Psalm 29
Car Talks

"Car talks" are where the difficult stuff gets discussed.
Usually the subjects of death and sex.
It is a challenge for the parent to stay on the road
and not drive into a ditch
when a kid expresses a thought that was unexpected.

It can be humorous.
Or it can be deadly serious.
Or it can be a combination of the two.

For example, my sick teenager says:

"I'm afraid, Mom."
*Oh, no, here it comes. Do we really have to discuss this
now? Ever?*
"What are you afraid of, honey?"
"I'm afraid of dying and missing the good stuff."
My eyes tear up, my throat is blocked by a lump as I
attempt to swallow my dread.
"What kind of stuff?"
I wager a guess…
"Things like driving, getting married, and having
kids?"
Without a moment of hesitation, he says,
"No. I'm afraid they are going to invent a great new
video game,
and I won't get to play it."

Or...

The time we drove home from his clinic appointment after hearing the doctor say that my child had only two months to live.
I couldn't choke my tears down that day.
It was hard to drive with a steady stream flowing down my cheeks.

What a surreal experience...
...discussing such things as cremation versus burial...
...who he wanted to give his prized possessions to...
...convincing him that his wishes mattered more than just considering the cost...
...dying in the hospital or calling hospice to assist us at home...

"I would really like you to be at home for the end, honey."

"I would rather be in the hospital, Mom. If I died at home, then afterwards, everyone would always pass that room and say,

'That is the room where my brother died.'"

Maybe, in the olden days, they had "buggy talks."
But I think cars come in pretty handy, sometimes.

Car Talks: Devotional

> But encourage one another day after day,
> as long as it is still called Today.
>
> —Hebrews 3:13 (NASB)

Talks in national parks can be pretty meaningful too.

Another *benefit* experienced by families affected by chronic illness is the serious, life-impacting conversations that somehow get waylaid if you feel you have forever or later to discuss them.

A meaningful but painful conversation between David and me happened while we were on a hike in Yosemite National Park. Everyone else with us that day had tromped way ahead. I lagged behind to walk with David, stopping occasionally while he had hacking coughing spasms.

We began talking about life expectancy, and he said, "We are both middle aged."

"How do you figure that?"

"Since you are forty-five years old and your life expectancy is maybe ninety, you're halfway there. And since I'm seventeen, and I think I will live to be forty years old. I'm almost halfway there."

So he figured we were both middle-aged.

It was a difficult talk. I had to bite my tongue to keep from lecturing him about doing his treatments more religiously. At the rate he was going, living to age 40 wasn't going to happen. I felt that making it to his high school graduation ten months away was going to be a challenge and a blessing if it happened.

Where have you had meaningful talks with your ill child? They often take us by surprise, so be aware. They are often painful, but they are also precious gifts.

Dear God,

Help me to be ever mindful
that a meaningful conversation
could take place anywhere, at any time.
Please give me wisdom and compassion
to listen and respond in a way that my child needs
at the time.
Thank You.

Amen.

Heart Psalm 30
There Are Worse Things

I hear of other families
whose children suffer
from a disease or condition
that is visible or disruptive in the extreme.

I say to my child,
"See, there are worse things to have
than what you have."

Can you believe I have said that?
Repeatedly?

How the heck do I know
what is better or worse?

I am on the outside
looking in.

How can I possibly know how it feels
to have a death sentence hanging over my head
every day of my life,
wondering if today will be the day my lung bleeds
and I drown in my own blood?

Or if I will contract a germ
that will run rampant and ravage my lungs,
antibiotics having little to no effect,
until they are so infected
that I can no longer draw another breath?

Or a dozen other things that can happen.

How can I possibly presume to know
the level of suffering of another human being?

I am close with my child.
But some things just can't be shared.

What a pity

and a blessing.

There Are Worse Things: Devotional

You have allowed me to suffer much hardship,
but you will restore me to life again and lift me up
from the depths of the earth.

—Psalm 71:20 (NLT)

I used to be obsessed with watching medical shows on
television. I would marvel at the medical miracles and
wonder about the lives of the unfortunate people, some who
lived in third-world countries, who had terrible, enormous
goiters, a conjoined twin, scar tissue from burns, crippled
limbs, or growths that would take over their faces or necks
or legs or backs.

Then there would be the reality shows that gave us a
glimpse of what life was like trying to raise a child who had
Tourette syndrome or schizophrenia or depression or drug
addiction. Those families never enjoyed a moment's rest.

And then I would find myself led down a path of Internet links that ended with pictures of beautiful, vibrant, active children, full of potential until struck down by a brain tumor or some such thing. On their way to their miniature graves, their treatments, including prednisone, bloated their precious bodies to unrecognizable proportions, their eyes just barely slits in their faces and muscle control so affected that they developed lazy eyes. Their once smiling, joyful faces now held only pain and suffering and confusion and waiting and longing for the inevitable to happen.

I couldn't help it. I would compare their lives with ours, and, being a natural optimist, I would find our lives coming out on top. The lucky ones.

After all, our child's disease's only outward signs were clubbed fingernails and toenails. You wouldn't notice it unless you were looking for it. And, of course, the smallness of stature for most because of malnutrition resulting from malabsorption of nutrients. And the barrel chests and hunched shoulders from the relentless, lifelong coughing, and the breathlessness and the restricted activities because of exhaustion. And the isolation because of the risk of catching other peoples' germs and getting sick and dying, and the scars from the multiple surgeries and procedures that were supposed to extend or enhance our child's life.

But besides those few little things, my kid is the "lucky one."

How dare I!

Do you ever forget that you will never know what it is like to live a day exactly like your child does? Unless you have the same disease, you and I cannot relate to our child on the same level. Just for today, I will try to accept my child and not compare his life with mine or anyone else's.

Dear God,

Please help me to be more compassionate.
Help me to hold my tongue
when my impulsive nature wants to take over
and paint sunshine and rainbows
all over the rain clouds on someone's day.
Others just need to be allowed to feel their feelings.
They are as valid as mine are.
Thank You, dear One who comforts us all.

Amen.

Our Story:
Just an Average Day

It is uncommon for me to have a calm or lazy day. Most of my days are hectic, with good moments in each one. But rarely is my worst, most chaotic day my best day. The following is an example of one day that turned out to be both.

The week before school started, David, age 13, and TJ, age 11, were admitted to the hospital due to complications from their CF. Kelsey turned sixteen years old while on a mission trip in Mexico with our church. When she arrived home on Saturday night, we washed her clothes and packed her back up to go to summer camp in the Santa Cruz Mountains the next day.

TJ was to begin the school year on Monday at a new school across town for gifted and talented (GATE) students. Since I wanted him to begin school with his class, I received permission from the doctor to bring him home from the hospital on Sunday night with his IV still in place. The three CF kiddos would have portacaths placed in their chests for their intravenous medications in the future, but at this point, they all had PICC lines in place. It is a long-term IV that can be hep-locked so the child is not tied to the IV pole between dosages. I was trained at the hospital in administrating his medications three times a day. Since I never had to puncture his skin, it wasn't as bad as I thought it would be. It was just time-consuming. And keeping my toddler away from the "new toys" (paraphernalia) was a chore.

I had to lay out all the syringes, six in all, *in order*, on a paper towel on the coffee table, after sterilizing it with alcohol. I needed always to be mindful of what my own hands touched. If they touched anything but a sterile item, I had to disinfect them again. No scratching my face or anything like that. I sure didn't want to be responsible for pumping germs into my child's blood stream and causing an infection.

So after church on Sunday morning, Tom took all the children in our fifteen-passenger van to Santa Cruz to deliver Kelsey to camp. I took off in the other direction to gather up TJ from the hospital. That night, while trying to get dinner served and cleaned up and trying to bathe the children and get their clothes laid out for their first day of school the next morning, guess what I discovered—lice!

"You have got to be kidding!" I said to myself as I ran to the store to buy the expensive boxes of lice shampoo. Upon my arrival home, my crying one-year-old baby wanted to be nursed and put to bed, but I couldn't oblige her until her hair was clean and clear, so I shampooed and combed out everyone, including myself—just to be safe.

The cranky baby was nursed and put down. I started TJ's first IV medication at 11:00 p.m., and it lasted about an hour. I laid the children out on the living room floor on a clean sheet to sleep for the night and started washing their bedding.

I finally got to bed at about 1:30 a.m. and rose at 5:00 a.m. to prepare and eat my breakfast and revive my spirit by reading my morning Bible devotion. Then another IV for TJ and a breathing treatment for him and McKenna, who was nine years old.

I got everyone up for breakfast and was grooming them while we waited for our neighbor to arrive to watch after Lynnsey, who was four years old, and Nina, the one-year-old. I then loaded up the van and drove Jordan, who was seven, and Shannon, who was six, and McKenna to their school and then ran TJ across town to his new school.

The principal and nurse were to meet with me at 8:30 a.m. to discuss the care of TJ's IV, but the nurse was delayed and wouldn't be available until 11:30 a.m. The principal didn't want TJ at school with an IV unless I was with him or until the nurse gave her approval, but my babysitter couldn't stay with my little ones past 9:30. So I supervised TJ in his classroom for an hour, and then we both dashed home to retrieve the toddlers.

Upon our arrival, the babysitter informed us that she could stay after all. As it turned out, I needed to get TJ's afternoon IV medications out of the refrigerator anyway, so I did that before rushing TJ back to school. (But not before an episode of separation anxiety from Lynnsey, who was screaming hysterically and gagging as I ran out the door.)

Until the nurse arrived, I had to follow TJ around the campus at recess and on his classroom's school tour. Can you imagine? Poor guy! I tried to blend in, hiding behind trees and generally remaining as inconspicuous as possible. I finally had a lengthy meeting with the nurse and principal, and then TJ and I went home after the minimum first day of school.

But I hadn't eaten since breakfast at 5:00 a.m. It was now 1:15, and I was starving. My meals are very important to me since I started my weight-loss program eight years earlier. So I nursed the baby to sleep and then prepared and ate my weighed and measured lunch.

Oh my! Had I forgotten to call David in the hospital to see how his day was? Yes! I dialed him up, and we talked while I ate.

Time for TJ's IV at 3:00 as the elementary-school children arrived home with tales of their new teachers, friends, classrooms, etc. And then I was reminded what else the children bring home on the first day of school—emergency forms! A minimum of four papers per child.

I *hate* filling out forms!

I still had to finish administering TJ's IVs and begin cooking dinner. I was petitioned an average of three times by each of the four scholars to *pleeease* fill out their forms because their teacher said they must return them, completed, the next day.

Exhaustion set in as I told them all, several times, that their teachers would have to understand because I couldn't possibly fill them out that night. Maybe I could get to them tomorrow. The children were crushed as they imagined trying to break the news to their new teachers. Perspective is a great teacher. In light of everything I was dealing with that night, the school forms were at the bottom of my priority list.

As I served up dinner, in staggered Tom. He had risen at 3:00 that morning, left the house at 3:30, and driven one and a half hours through bumper-to-bumper traffic to his job as a truck driver foreman, as he did four days a week. He oversaw the truck drivers, as well as drove the most demanding route on most days. I imagine he would have wanted to eat dinner, shower, and fall into bed.

I was quickly approaching my physical and emotional threshold as I cleaned the kitchen and prepared the next day's lunches. Then I heard the children talking with their dad in the living room. This is when my worst day turned into my best day.

As I prepared TJ's evening IV medications, Tom walked past me with a pen and gathered up all the dreaded school forms. He looked like an angel with a shimmering halo and a five o'clock shadow. Through bleary eyes, aching muscles, and creaking joints, he took on the task that I could not force myself to face. Not that night.

I was so relieved I could have cried. He didn't *ask* me if I wanted him to do it. I didn't have to ask, wouldn't have *thought* of asking. He just knew it would be a precious gift to me.

The next time we passed by each other, I thanked him and told him that that was the most romantic thing he had ever done. I have yet to adequately thank him. We'll have to make an appointment. Pencil me in for a week from next Friday.

The day was not far off that I learned to do home IVs on two and then three children at the same time. Woohoo!

The lesson?

Nurses work in shifts for a reason!

Prayers, Notes, Reflections

_____
_____
_____
_____
_____
_____
_____
_____
_____
_____
_____
_____
_____
_____
_____
_____
_____
_____
_____
_____
_____
_____
_____
_____
_____
_____

6

I Don't Believe in Accidents

Heart Psalm 31
Brutal Transparency: It Isn't for Sissies

Do you really want to know?
No.
You do not.

You ask,
"How are you? How is your child?
How are things going?"

I could answer in volumes.
But what you really want to hear is,
"Fine. We're all fine."

What would you do if I answered in full detail?

Do you really want to hear the latest medical report?
Do you really want to hear about how we struggle
and suffer?

No, you would wait for the earliest opportunity to
bow out and rush away.

Can I bear to say, out loud, what is really going on,
anyway?
Or will just uttering the words and releasing them
into the atmosphere
make them more threatening? More real? More true?

Can my mouth actually form the words?
Can I make my breath push the words past the
lump in my throat
and out into the air to assault your ear?

I can hardly bear it.

And you *surely* cannot bear it.

So I swallow my tears.
I say everything is going fine.
We hug, and I walk away.

Perhaps saying "everything is fine" will make it true.

Can you handle it?
Brutal transparency?

Brutal Transparency: Devotional

Give all your worries and cares to God,
for he cares about you.

—1 Peter 5:7 (NLT)

It is hard to find a friend who is close enough to *unload* on.
We don't want to overburden anyone, but the truth is, we
can be pretty needy.

Parents of chronically ill children—we have a lot going
on emotionally, as well as all the planning, scheduling, and
general running of a home and family. We don't want to

overwhelm our friends, but we struggle for our sanity when things get intense.

It can be a challenge to get out of our own head and situation to remember that our friends have their "stuff" too. They have their families, spouses, jobs, and homes to manage.

While I was going through a particularly trying time, a friend sat down with me at a church function and got down and dirty with me, asking in-depth questions and sharing my grief with tears of her own. She really cared about me, and she backed up her newfound knowledge about our family's situation with action. She got together a group of women to help to make our holidays that year especially meaningful and less stressful for us.

I am trying to remember, when a friend asks me about my life, to give a brief answer and then make sure to ask her about her family. It is my effort to reciprocate the friendship and not get completely caught up in my own cares.

Dear God,

Teach me how to be a good friend.
I want to be a support for my friends,
as well as being on the receiving end.
I would like things to be more *equal* or *even*.
I don't want to seem so needy.
Grow my shoulders strong enough
for my friends to lean on.
Help me to help carry others' burdens

as they help me carry mine.
Thank You, precious Savior.

Amen.

Heart Psalm 32
It's Inevitable, So Why Bother?

I saw a movie. The premise:
No matter what you do,
what is supposed to happen
will happen.

There is nothing you can do about it.
Even if you try to manipulate events,
you may be, in fact, causing the very thing
you were trying to keep from happening.

I think that is how my sick child thinks.

He didn't watch the movie with us.
But I think, if he had, he would have exclaimed,
"You see, I'm not the only one who thinks this way."

Who's to say what's true? If my son is right,
there is very little use in doing
all his prescribed treatments.
Just do what helps him feel better immediately.
Nothing more.

If he is wrong, he is robbing himself of many
precious years of life.

It does no good for me to try to reason with him.
The conversations are extraordinarily painful and
utterly fruitless.

"Your treatments are not a curse," I say.
"People with other diseases pray for
medications and therapies
to extend their lives," I state.

I am talking to a wall.
I am not him. And he is not me.
I love him and must accept his way of thinking.

So I climb off his back.
Let him be.
I stop being his doctor.
I will just be his mom
and his friend.

What was meant to happen
will happen.

Right?

It's Inevitable: Devotional

There is more hope for a fool than for someone
who speaks without thinking.

—Proverbs 29:20 (NLT)

"You've lost 28 pounds since your last clinic visit three months ago," said my son's pulmonary specialist. "That puts you down 48 pounds from your all-time high of 180." The doctor looked to my son for a reaction but got none.

"Do you have anything to say about all of this?" he asked.

"I haven't been feeling well. I've been nauseated, so I can't eat."

"Besides the weight issue, David, you won't blow in the spirometer."

"I can't take deep breaths without coughing really bad."

The doctor looked down and made some notations in David's chart, which, over the past seventeen years, has grown to over two inches thick.

"What do you do each day to take care of your health?"

David thought about it for a moment. "I do nebulized Albuterol two to four times a day, Pulmozyme once every morning, Tobi twice per day every other month. I take my Paxil and Prilosec every night and my enzymes—five capsules with each meal, four with snacks. I do my percussion vest two to four times per day and my tube feeding every night."

The doctor made more notes in David's chart, then asked, "Have you been doing your Advair?"

David rolled his eyes. "No."

The doctor looked up from David's chart. "Why not?"

David gave him a blank stare.

I quietly answered for him. "It tastes bad, so he doesn't like to do it."

The doctor looked back at his paperwork and jotted down some more notes.

"And have you been doing your hypertonic saline solution?"

David looked at the floor. "No."

"Why not?"

David hesitated. "I just don't feel like it does any good."

"Are you doing your Colistin?"

"No. We don't have any in the house."

"Yes we do, David," I said softly. "You just wouldn't do it when I mixed it up because it also tastes bad. It ended up getting thrown away."

David's eyes shot darts at me.

"Are you taking your Megace?"

"No."

"Why not?"

Another icy stare.

This little exchange was repeated again and again as the doctor asked David if he was taking his vitamins, Zithromax, and Reglan. I could tell that, even behind his protective surgical mask, the doctor was angry, disheartened. Here was a patient, *his* patient, who was doing only about half of his prescribed treatments and was suffering the dire consequences of his actions.

The doctor quietly exploded in frustration. "You're doing nothing, David. Nothing!"

As parents, we can feel as if we are between a rock and a hard place when dealing with our sick child and his medical team. We need to seek wisdom during such times.

Holy moly, God!

Please show me and my child compassion.
Thank You.

Amen.

Prayers, Notes, Reflections

Heart Psalm 33
Words

Words are just words.
But why do we put such stock in each word
our child's doctor utters
to describe our child's progress, or lack thereof?

Don't they know that we live our lives
counting down the weeks, days, hours
before the next clinic visit?

We tub and scrub our child.
We memorize what medications he takes
and what foods he eats.

We rearrange our busy schedules,
plan child care for the siblings,
pack food to take with us,
and prepare meals for the children at home.

We drive several hours,
wait in the play room,
and then finally it is our turn
to see the esteemed doctor.

We take mental notes of their precise words
so we can repeat them, *exactly*,
to our friends and relatives
when we recap our child's appointment.

"Children who are as sick as your child is
get listed for transplant,"
the doctor utters nonchalantly
as he exits the room.

Transplant!

The very word hits me square in the chest,
forcing the breath out of my lungs
and threatening to suffocate me.
At once, I am dizzy. My stomach lurches,
and I fear I will vomit.

To the doctor,
it is just a word in his occupational vocabulary,
tossed about so flippantly
and easily forgotten
as he moves on to his next patient.

To me, it means the approach of death.
To others, it is life.

Words.
They are so meaningful.

Words: Devotional

Pleasant words are a honeycomb.
Sweet to the soul and healing to the bones.

—Proverbs 16:24 (NASB)

Words have the power to hurt or to heal. I have always been injured easily by other people's words. When our medical staff speaks to us in their everyday, medical language, it is normal to them, but it can be shocking to us lay people, especially when we have so much at stake: our child's very life and well being.

I guess I should let them off the hook. Perhaps words don't mean as much to other people as they do to me. And besides, this is my life—or rather, the life of my child. It is just the doctor's occupation.

Does that excuse his callousness? Is it possible or desirable to expect our doctor to feel the impact that his words have on his patients or their families?

What would happen to the medical staff if they didn't distance themselves emotionally from their patients? Perhaps they don't have proper training in *bedside manner*. Maybe they should.

Regardless, as a parent of a chronically ill child, I have to grow a thick skin. It does no good to get hurt feelings or let an injury fester. I have to forgive and get past it, consider that it wasn't an intentional slight or jab.

> Lord, let me learn through my experiences,
> to be gentle with others in all regards.
> Let my thoughts, words, and actions (TWA)
> be honoring to You
> and a balm to hurting people.
> Thank You, Lord.
>
> Amen.

Prayers, Notes, Reflections

Heart Psalm 34
Finding Meaning in the Disease

My child asks…
"Why do I have this disease?"
"Why me and not someone else?"
"Why is my life so hard?"
"Why do I have to live with pain and embarrassment?"

I wonder…
"Why does my family have to go through all this?"
"Why does my child suffer?"
"Will a cure be found?"
"How long can we go on like this?"

We both say…
"I HATE YOU, DISEASE!"
"GO AWAY!"
"What good are you to me or my family?"

And then the answers come.

After years of wrestling with the disease,
my child says to me…

"Mom, I know why I have this disease.
I know what my life purpose is."

I am curious.
A profound moment is quickly approaching,
and here it is:

"I have this disease so
I can be aware of God's goodness every day.
And so I can meet other people with this disease
and tell them about God.
My faith is much stronger because of my disease.
My disease has helped to shape me,
helped me to develop my values.
It has played a big part
in who I am.
I am glad I have this disease."

I am astounded!

God is so good to speak to my child,
and thus, to me.

Finding Meaning in the Disease: Devotional

It was good for me to be afflicted
so that I might learn your decrees.
I know, O Lord,
that your laws are righteous,
and in faithfulness
you have afflicted me.

—Psalm 119:71, 75 (NIV)

My child's band traveled to Dayton, Ohio, for world
championships. I went along as a chaperone. While there,
David and I had an extraordinary conversation.

The rest of the students went on a side trip to the air museum, and David and I were resting in our hotel room. We were chatting about nothing in particular, and somehow we ended up talking about his illness. Throughout the course of the conversation, David said the following:

"I'm glad I have CF. It has helped to shape my belief system and my ideals. It is a part of me, and I'm glad I have it. What's the worst that could happen? I could die sooner, but since I know that I am going to heaven, that's not the worst thing that could happen. It is the best thing! The most important thing is to take as many people with me as possible."

This statement thrilled me, but later, it would also petrify me. I was comforted by the fact that David felt secure in his eternity, but I was also to learn that it can be used to surrender, like, *Why bother to stay healthy? I know I am going to heaven anyway, so why struggle so hard?*

Have you been blessed to discover a deep heart conversation with your child sneaking up on you? These moments cannot be planned. They are spontaneous gifts from God. Don't forget to express your gratitude to Him for his many blessings each day.

Dear God,

You are so good to give me a glimpse
inside my child's heart.
You have made him tender and insightful.
I am in awe of how You compensate my sick children.

Yes, they lack good health,
but, in return,
You have gifted them with
extraordinary understanding.
Thank You endlessly.

Amen.

Heart Psalm 35
That Fateful Day

One autumn day, our child's doctor
told us that our child would likely die
in two months.

Will my child live until Christmas?
I wondered.

Yes, he lived.

But, now, every occasion,
every holiday that approaches,

I ask:

Will this be my child's last birthday?
Will this be my child's last Easter?
Will this be my child's last Thanksgiving?

The last movie he will see?

His last haircut?

His last breath?

His last everything?

My way of thinking has changed forever.

That Fateful Day: Devotional

Do not boast about tomorrow.
For you do not know
what a day may bring forth.

—Proverbs 27:1 (NASB)

Our family has lived through several "fateful days" with our sick children. Besides McKenna's cancer scare and subsequent surgery, she has developed serious cystic fibrosis-related diabetes (CFRD), which has been nearly impossible to control. She has had a few life-threatening high blood sugars, as well as lows, on a nearly daily basis.

McKenna and TJ have both experienced mild lung bleeds that are terribly unnerving, as we never know, when they are happening, if they are mild or will continue until the child bleeds to death. One of McKenna's bleeds was a slow leak that went on for days. It was making me a nervous wreck. She ended up in the hospital, where I thought she would be well taken care of.

Unfortunately, a safety precaution was not observed, and McKenna nearly coded out. It turns out that she is allergic to infused Vitamin K. She had an anaphylactic reaction. The nurse was out of the room when McKenna's throat swelled, her temperature spiked, and she instantly broke out in a rash. I was to find out later that when administering a new medication, the patient should not be left alone, even for a while, for this exact reason.

During David's worst downward spiral, he became so ill that I was convinced he would surely die right in front of my eyes. I was afraid to leave his side for even a moment, lest he would slip away alone.

Because of all these health issues, I don't go in to see if my children are awake and getting ready for school each morning. I go in to see if they are still breathing, still alive.

Do most mothers go through this on a daily basis? It feels insane!

I need God to uphold me in His loving arms every day. Have you had days in which you would surely hit the floor if God didn't uphold you? Make sure to call on Him, for He cares for you.

> Well, God,
>
> You know that *I* even had
> a fateful day of my own.
> During my simple appendectomy,
> the doctor nicked my aorta,
> and he nearly couldn't save me.
> So we truly don't know
> what each day holds for any of us.
> I'm thankful that I can trust You
> to hold me
> and all of my family members
> in the palm of Your hand.
>
> Amen.

Prayers, Notes, Reflections

_____

_____

_____

_____

_____

_____

_____

_____

_____

_____

_____

_____

_____

_____

_____

_____

_____

_____

_____

_____

_____

_____

_____

_____

Heart Psalm 36
I'm Sooo Tired

My schedule has been packed.
No time to rest.

I'm so tired.
I don't know if I can eat my next meal.
(but I know I will)

If I blink my eyes,
I don't think I will be able to raise the lids again.
(oh…there…I did it!)

I think I could sleep for a week.
(but, of course, I won't.)

Things need to get done!

We had surprise visitors at our house today.
Oh! What an embarrassment!
No warning to launch us into a ten-minute
"spring cleaning."

Now they think we live like this
all the time.

I hate that!

I actually had the downstairs clean
just two days ago, believe it or not.
What happened with that?

I imagine everyone else
lives in houses that look like model homes.

Do you?

I'm Sooo Tired: Devotional

Come to Me, all who are weary and heavy laden,
and I will give you rest.

—Matthew 11:28 (NASB)

Several years ago, when I was still perpetually pregnant and
dealing with morning sickness, my husband, Tom, worked
nights. One morning, while I was lying on the couch, trying
not to puke, Tom was sleeping. Our two preschool age kids
were playing in the backyard of our downstairs apartment
when, wouldn't you know it, a family member came to pay
us a surprise visit. I dragged my sorry self off the couch to
answer the door and was astonished and deeply embarrassed
to see our visitors with my two little tykes in tow.

Apparently, there was a breach in our fence behind
some bushes, and the kids had escaped just in time for our
relatives to catch them in the parking lot before any harm
came to them. I was so grateful and relieved until they
unleashed a stern lecture on us for our irresponsibility and
poor parenting skills.

It was one of those moments you wish you didn't have to live through but will hopefully learn from…about how *not* to treat others.

It certainly was an unsafe situation for our little ones, but it would have been nice if, instead of lecturing us for our atrocious parenting skills, they had taken a moment to remember we were good parents, and that this was an unusual incident.

And what if they had listened to how it happened and, finding out we were exhausted, had offered to take the kids for the afternoon while we took a much-needed nap? Heaven! And maybe too much to hope for.

My prayer for parents of young children is this: May you get twice the rest with half the sleep.

Dear Lord,

Please teach me through my experiences.
Make me tender-hearted.
Remind me to see and meet the needs of others
instead of condemning them.
Thank You.

Amen.

Our Story:
TJ's Accident

The children were playing outside. Tom and I were in our living room, repairing a bicycle. I remember the date (Monday, January 31) because we were watching news reports about an Alaskan airliner that had crashed off the coast of Santa Barbara. A friend of ours flew for that airline, and we were concerned for his safety.

As I glanced out our big picture window that faced the street, I casually asked Tom, "Did TJ just jump out of that tree, or did he fall?" We had a peach tree in the corner of our front yard, and part of it grew over the sidewalk that was hidden from us by a hedgerow.

Tom hadn't seen anything, but since TJ (age 9) hadn't reappeared, we nonchalantly walked out to the front yard to investigate. As we approached the place where TJ lay, Tom yelled for me to get the phone and call 911. TJ was unconscious and wasn't breathing. Apparently, he *had* fallen. Eight feet. Onto cement. On his head.

I ran to the house to make the call, and Tom began mouth-to-mouth resuscitation. By this time, the neighbors began to assemble, and the kids all came running to see what was happening.

In a matter of minutes, a fire engine arrived, and the professionals took over TJ's emergency care. They cut his clothes off and took his vital statistics. He was breathing on his own by then, but he stopped several more times that evening, and he didn't regain consciousness.

If humor could be found in any situation, my twisted, optimistic mind would find it. Just that morning, TJ had put on some old pants with big holes in the knees to wear to school, but I scolded him and had him change into his new pair.

After I left in the ambulance with TJ, Tom gathered up the ruined clothes. It included his new pants, *without* holes in the knees. Darn it anyway!

Our across-the-street neighbor took in all our children for several hours while Tom drove to Children's Hospital to join me in the emergency department and then up to the critical care unit.

I, on the other hand, was on my first ambulance ride. While en route, TJ stopped breathing a couple of times and had to be resuscitated again. I rode in the front with the driver and answered questions about TJ's health history.

Upon arriving at the hospital and meeting up with Tom, we were ushered into the family room to await the news about our son's condition. About a half an hour later, we were introduced to Dr. Betts. He was familiar to us because he had been on television and became quite famous a few years earlier when the Loma Prieta earthquake knocked down the Cypress structure, a freeway in the San Francisco Bay Area.

Dr. Betts had crawled into perilous situations to help save some trapped patients. He freed some of them by amputating limbs, sometimes nearly blindly, in order to save their lives. It was a grizzly state of affairs, which was probably the reason we remembered him.

Dr. Betts explained to us that TJ had broken his shoulder, cracked his skull, was bleeding into his brain, which had been bruised, and had a concussion. He was on medication to keep him unconscious because whenever he began to regain consciousness, he became combative, which was common with brain injuries. But whenever he lost consciousness, he would stop breathing. So machines were keeping him breathing in the meantime.

It would be several hours or days before we would know if TJ would be permanently brain damaged or paralyzed, the doctor said, so they had him hooked up to all kinds of machinery and on several medications to stabilize him for the time being.

Tom and I decided I would stay with TJ through the night, and Tom would go home to care for the other children. He would also call our families, our pastor, and his work and explain the need to be excused for several days until the crisis passed, *if* it passed.

I didn't sleep at all that night. TJ was restrained in his bed, but he thrashed about occasionally. He couldn't really wake up, but I noticed he *could* feel pain. I don't know why they didn't put a permanent catheter in because they had to keep inserting a temporary one to empty his bladder. Each time this was done, it was very disturbing to TJ.

Besides the catheter and all the wires connected all over his chest, TJ had tubes going in his mouth and nose. One of them was connected to a suction machine to empty his stomach, but it didn't work because late during the night, TJ vomited all the pizza he had eaten for dinner that night and was choking. The relief nurse was the only nurse there, and she was older and wasn't strong enough to move TJ to change his sheets, so I had to help clean up the smelly mess after she suctioned his mouth and throat.

Since the staff was aware that TJ had cystic fibrosis, the doctor ordered a breathing treatment for him. That was fine, but they also ordered a vest treatment. The vest fills with air, and it rhythmically percusses the lungs to loosen the mucus that clogs the airways. We had one at home that the kids regularly used.

But I had to remind the staff that it was an inappropriate treatment at that time, given the fact that TJ's shoulder was broken and he had a head injury. They were causing him considerable pain just trying to get the contraption on him, much less shake him half to death. I was learning, ever so slowly, to advocate for my kids. It was a tricky business which, regretfully, we failed to adequately teach the children.

TJ and I made it through the night. In the morning, Tom and I agreed that he would get the kids off to school, and then he would drive to the hospital. When he arrived,

I would go home to eat lunch, prepare and pack my dinner and breakfast, and get the kids home from school. Then Tom's parents would come over for an hour while I drove back to the hospital to spell Tom. We did this all week.

On my first trip home, I walked out to the place TJ had fallen. I noticed a broken branch on the ground. When I looked up, I understood what had happened.

TJ had climbed out on a branch that was too small to support his weight, and it broke, spilling him onto the sidewalk on his head and shoulder. If given the opportunity, I would have a talk with TJ, explaining about tree-climbing safety.

While I ate my meals in the family waiting room at the hospital during the next few days, I got to know another mom who had a three-year-old son on the ward. I found out that a television had fallen on her son's head while her husband slept on the sofa nearby.

The toddler was trying to change the video. The TV, which sat atop a wobbly table, tumbled over on top of him. She was out of the house at the time. She was also five months pregnant with their second child. We ate our meals together and talked about our children and pregnancies. We became friends.

During Tom's second day at the hospital, he called me with news that TJ had regained consciousness. This was wonderful news. He was talking and was conversational. His brain seemed to be working normally. Hallelujah!

The next day, also while Tom was there in the afternoon, he called me and said that TJ wanted to use the bathroom. They took out the catheter and gave him a bedpan, but TJ wanted to walk to the bathroom. The staff was hesitant but allowed him to try.

With nurses on each side, TJ walked down the hall to the restroom, did his business, and walked back to his bed. Jubilation! He was not paralyzed!

He made steady progress for the next three days and was discharged on Friday afternoon with referrals to see several doctors over the next week. We were also given some paperwork to take to the hospital in Hayward where the medical records were kept. TJ was fitted for a harness to immobilize his arm with the broken shoulder and was instructed to wear it twenty-four hours a day until cleared by the orthopedic surgeon. He would visit numerous doctors many times in the coming months.

On our way home from the hospital, we stopped at the medical office in Hayward. When TJ and I walked in the front door, we ran into the mom of the toddler from the ward. She was walking in with a couple of family members. As we hugged, I asked her how her son was doing.

"He died this morning."

I was stunned and visibly shaken. How could this have happened? I suddenly felt guilty that my son was recovering and walking next to me while her son was lying in the morgue. We hugged again, and she said that she had details that she had to deal with, so we parted ways, but I could hardly see where I was going through my tears.

TJ did recover fully, with only periodic bouts of vertigo and headaches that faded completely after a period of two years. It is noteworthy to mention that as soon as TJ got out of the car at our house after being released from the hospital, he climbed directly up the tree that was outside his car door.

But he learned his lesson when he jumped down. It really jarred his broken shoulder. It didn't stop Tom, however, from vowing to cut down every tree in the neighborhood. I tried to convince him that children needed to climb trees, even and especially TJ. We would just have to keep relying on guardian angels.

So although TJ would always have his chronic illness of cystic fibrosis and would develop the chronic illness of diabetes, we didn't have to deal with other chronic conditions such as paralysis or brain injury. We are eternally grateful that TJ's story turned out so well.

Prayers, Notes, Reflections

7

WHAT'S MOST IMPORTANT

Heart Psalm 37
That's Not Fair!

It's true.
There are many things in life that aren't fair.
Our kids have *the advantage*
of learning that lesson early in their lives.

Some of our children
have several hours of
health maintenance to perform each day.

They have blood tests, shots, IVs,
finger pokes, daily insulin injections,
hospital stays, port flushes,
surgeries, procedures.
They miss events because they are ill.

The same children get to eat,
have to eat,
a lot of special food each day.
They get extra toys to play with
while in the hospital.

The "well children" have to do more chores
because the ill children
don't have the time or stamina.

"It's just not fair!"

That's right, it's not.

It's not fair for the well children or the ill ones.
So deal with it.

There are many, many things in life
that don't seem fair.
Our children have daily *opportunities*
to learn that lesson at an early age.

What a mixed blessing.

That's Not Fair!: Devotional

"The Lord gave and the Lord has taken away.
Blessed be the name of the Lord."
Through all this Job did not sin nor did he blame God.

—Job 1:21–22 (NASB)

Isn't it odd? We avoid hardship like the plague, yet the difficult experiences cause us to grow the most. Dealing with unfairness isn't easy, but what else can we do? Our children are not the same as one another.

We don't like to compare or label—sick kid, well kid. But facts are facts. Different kids have different needs, abilities, talents, and personalities. We have to work with what we've got. We do the best we can.

And, no, it doesn't *seem* fair. In fact, it *isn't* fair—the workload, the toy and snack distribution, the disappointment, and the pain. Not to mention the time and attention that seems lopsidedly doled out. But that's the way it is. It's a tough lesson for *adults* to learn, nearly impossible for *children* to accept.

But when they do, it will benefit them in their adult lives. They will live with injustices in and out of the workplace. They will meet people who lack integrity. They will be cheated and come across people who get ahead by dishonest means. We can hope that the training they endured by living in our family will come back to benefit them.

Do you have children who are in good health? Do you juggle schedules, medications, dietary needs, and attention for both sick and well kids and still face resentment? It is very tricky to do and difficult to explain to small children. Turn to God. He will give you the strength, wisdom, and patience to get through each day.

Dear Lord,

Please grant me wisdom and kindness
as I deal with life's unfairness with our children.
Help them to have compassion toward one another.
Teach me to have a tender spirit
and not to ignore our children's feelings,
even in the midst of busyness and chaos.
Let them learn from their experiences
and be better people because of them.
Thank You.

Amen.

Prayers, Notes, Reflections

Heart Psalm 38
This is Progress?

Children make progress in their education.
Technology makes progress.
City planners make progress in their towns.
Transportation makes progress.
Building businesses is considered progress.
A politician wins her office because she is considered
"progressive."
Physical training for athletes has progressed.

Progress is good!

Yes?

NO!
Progress is *not always* good!

If your child has a progressive disease,

Progress is not good!!!

NO!

Progress means more loss of function.

It means pain!

It means fear!

It means death!

REVERSE THE PROGRESS!!!

This is Progress: Devotional

Two are better than one because they have a good
return for their labor.
If one falls, the one will lift up his companion...
A cord of three strands is not quickly torn apart.

—Ecclesiastes 4:9, 10, and 12 (NASB)

Before the children were released from one of their hospitalizations, they were all diagnosed with cystic fibrosis-related diabetes (CFRD). What a drag! CFRD is not treatable with diet or pills, only by insulin injections.

The boys were more or less borderline, but McKenna needed several insulin injections each day. Of course, she would not give herself her shot. She would only draw up the insulin in the syringe. The nurses administered her shots while trying to educate and train her before she was released from the hospital.

When she got home, I gave the shots, though I never would have imagined I could. But in all honesty, with my diminishing eyesight due to increasing age, I could barely see the tiny needle. And since McKenna drew up the insulin, it worked out fine. It occurred to me that my own gestational diabetes was on-the-job training for what lay ahead.

After being home for a couple of weeks, McKenna wanted to go away with a group from church for four days, so she had to learn to do her own shots if she were to go.

I had my doubts whether or not it would happen, but she surprised us all. McKenna, who wouldn't swallow a pill or spit in a cup (to give a sputum sample, necessary for culturing lung bugs so the proper antibiotic could be prescribed), was giving herself injections! And they say there is no God!

Then David and TJ came home from their next hospitalization being insulin dependent. They now give themselves injections like McKenna. Well, sometimes McKenna does David's for him when he is especially tired. It is sweet to see her caring for him in that way. Unbelievable, actually. She still won't take pills or spit in a cup, but she learned to inject herself and her brother. Amazing to see.

Progress can go both ways at the same time. Our children's disease is progressing, but their personal growth is also progressing.

> Dear God,
>
> it is clear that Your ways are not my ways.
> I would not allow my children to go through life's trials
> if it were up to me.
> But I know that hardships develop my kids' character
> and cause personal, spiritual, and emotional growth,
> which they need in order to grow up and mature.
> Thank You for not letting me be in charge.
> Thank You for doing Your job,
> even when I rebel against it and You.
> You and Your works are awesome to behold!
>
> Amen!

Prayers, Notes, Reflections

Heart Psalm 39
The Roller Coaster

Things can change so quickly.
The day can begin so wonderfully,
and in an instant, the peace is shattered.

A child can wake up with a severe fever.

Or someone may begin vomiting.

Or I realize that someone hasn't eaten for a few days.

Or someone wakes up with blood on her mouth
and pillowcase...

...during the night, her coughing had brought on
a nightmarish lung bleed.

Or hysterical yelling comes from a bathroom...

...a teen reporting that his insides are coming out
his bottom.

Or someone's cough becomes incessant.

Or a child can't breathe.

All at once, I begin to tremble on the inside,
and I fear I will scream.

Please, let me off this ride!

But, no. On the outside, I am a pillar,
the calm in the midst of the storm.

I am mistaken for someone who is callous,
hard-hearted, insensitive.

And that is how I feel sometimes.

Because *someone* has to be in control,
to call the advice nurse,

to drive to the emergency room,
to manage the crisis.
Then the roller coaster takes a welcome turn.
The doctor prescribes a medication that works miraculously.
The sick child may be admitted to the hospital, where trained nurses take over.
Or the answer is simple; I just couldn't think clearly.
Or someone offers a helping hand.
Or the fever breaks.
The cough is calmed. The child sleeps.

I take a deep breath…in and out.

A little one hugs my neck,

and I hear, *I love you, Mommy,*

whispered in my ear.

I get a good night's sleep.

I get up early to read my devotions, write in my journal, and eat my breakfast in peace.

My serenity is restored.

Relative normalcy returns.

I go on with my day and my life with the knowledge that the roller coaster never stops.
There are no guarantees of what lies ahead
or just around the bend.

Today is a new day,
and it holds its own surprises.

Wheeee!

The Roller Coaster: Devotional

> Trust in the Lord with all your heart,
> and do not depend on your own understanding.
> Seek His will in all you do,
> And He will show you which path to take.
>
> —Proverbs 3:5–6 (NLT)

Don'tcha just love it?

You have your day all planned out. You have all the preparations ready. All the laundry is washed, dried, folded, *and* put away. Everything is in its place and accounted for (a rare occurrence). Nothing can go wrong.

And then, *bam!*

Wow! I didn't see *that* coming! I guess I should have learned by now that plans are not foolproof. I can plan all I want, and things can still go awry. It is true with life in general. When you have a child or two, even more so. When you have a *sick kid*, absolutely!

Does this happen to you? Our kids get sick mostly on Friday evenings or while on vacation when communication with our doctor is difficult or impossible. Why is that? Because it is the most inconvenient, that's why. I know, I know, they can't help it and didn't plan it, but we still have to deal with it.

It can seem as if our child's birth certificate is more like a ticket for the scariest ride at the amusement park. Some people like those rides. I would rather sit on a bench and watch people walk by sometimes. Life can get pretty exciting, and I would prefer a breather.

Do you ever feel that way? Do the unexpected events in your day overwhelm you? Especially if they weren't scheduled into your weekly planner. They are more opportunities to trust God. Hang on and enjoy the ride!

> Dear Lord,
>
> You know that sometimes if I don't laugh,
> I will just sit down and cry.
> Please be with me and give me wisdom, strength, and compassion
> to deal with each situation, with each child, in a way that will honor You.
> Thank You.
>
> Amen.

Heart Psalm 40
No Matter What

Some people believe
that children
who are not "perfect" or "normal"
are not deserving of life.

If you can't contribute to society,
what good are you?

I choose to believe what God says:
Children are a blessing.
Children are valuable.
All children have worth.

No matter what may be "wrong" with them,
all children are precious.
They are a precious gift from God.

Each child has a purpose.
They bring joy into our lives.

They teach us lessons
that we otherwise would not have learned.

How to be grateful.
How not to take things for granted.
How to love more.
To live every day to the fullest.

No Matter What: Devotional

I am fearfully and wonderfully made.

—Psalm 139:14 (NASB)

It isn't just our "sick" kids who seem to have something wrong with them. My "well" kids can cause me as much anxiety and grief as the "sick" ones. Here's one thing I learned, though, about venting my frustration:

Remember who you are talking to—and be sensitive.

Here's what happened:

I was complaining to a friend about one of my well children's character flaws. We had recently experienced a disturbing incident with her, nothing life-threatening or illegal, just bothersome and irritating. So I was venting to my friend, when all of a sudden, she burst into tears. Between sobs, she said, "Just love her! Love her and appreciate her while you still can!"

What a dope I am!

Why didn't I take into account that *her* daughter had just died of her chronic illness two months earlier? Her daughter and my daughter had been childhood friends. She didn't have a daughter anymore, and I still did, no matter how imperfect.

And she was exactly right. We are all flawed—me, especially. Until we each become perfected, we need to tolerate each other's flaws and love and appreciate each other while we still can.

> Thank you, God,
> for each of my dear children.
> No matter what is "wrong" with them
> or what they do wrong,
> all my children are Your gifts to me,
> and I am grateful.
> Help me to love and appreciate each of them every day.
> Thank You.
>
> Amen.

Prayers, Notes, Reflections

Heart Psalm 41
The Imposter: Me

People say they are impressed.
They "take their hat off to me."
They say, "I don't know how you do it,"
"You are amazing,"
"You must surely be organized."

Why?

I guess I toot my own horn sometimes.
I like them to be impressed.
I want them to think I am amazing.
I tell them my busy schedule
so they can look at me
and shake their heads in wonder.

But they don't know.

They don't see that my house is always in disarray.
They don't know that I lay awake at night
and wonder how I will get through another day
and if I am doing the right thing.
I'm second-guessing my every decision.

They don't know that when I pray,
I don't always feel it will do any good.
They don't know the uncertainty I live with.
They don't feel the discouragement
or the panic that rises during crisis.

But I do.

And I feel like a fraud.
I let people think I'm supermom.
I let them think I'm super spiritual
because I get up early every morning
to do my devotions, journaling,
and eat my healthy breakfast in peace.

I wear two faces.

Which one is me?

The Imposter: Me: Devotional

But let everyone be quick to hear,
slow to speak and slow to anger.

—James 1:19 (NASB)

It was an unusual day.

My kitchen was clean, the dishwasher was running, and
all the beds were made. All the toys were in the toy box.
The books were standing up in the shelf, and the folded
clothes were neatly piled in the dresser drawers. I felt proud
and victorious!

Then I realized I was sitting on the couch, watching the
big purple dinosaur all by myself. Where had my toddlers
and preschoolers disappeared to?

Oh no. I heard giggling coming from the bedroom—reason enough for suspicion and terror to strike the heart of every parent. I went to investigate.

Here they are.

Oh no!

I was aghast! They were in the process of throwing every toy, every book, every piece of clothing, and *all* the bedding, including the pillows, *out their large window and into the yard*!

Aaarrrgghhh! What could have possessed them to do this? Why, why, why!

What would you do in this situation? Here is all I could think of doing:

I took them each by the hand—not very gently, I might add. I sat them down on their naked beds and told them, very quietly (through gritted teeth), not to move or make a sound until I came back.

Then I went to the kitchen, grabbed the phone, and called my grandmother. "I'm gonna kill 'em!"

The funniest thing is that, after I spilled my story, Grandma told me this was not the first phone call of its kind she had ever received. Three decades earlier, her daughter (my aunt) had called her from across the street, where she lived, and said, "If you don't come and get my oldest daughter, I'm gonna kill her!" She had just cut off her little sister's long curly hair.

We laughed, and after I hung up, I took the kids out to the backyard and helped them pick everything up, push it all back through the window, and put it away.

So now ya know. I guess none of us are perfect or super spiritual. Or maybe *you* are, and it is just *my* family that is a phone call away from committing homicide on a daily basis. (Kidding! Please don't call Children's Protective Services on me!)

It's hard to be so honest. I don't like to face certain things about myself, much less discuss them in public. But it's true—I am selfish and impatient. I am egotistical. I have delusions of grandeur. I want the accolades. I am *so* imperfect. But more and more, I want to be like Jesus.

> Dear Lord,
>
> Please take away more of me
> and replace it with You.
> May my every TWA (**t**hought, word, action)
> honor You
> each moment of every day.
> Thank You.
>
> Amen.

Heart Psalm 42
A Vanilla World

A life without adversity
would be like an ice cream parlor
offering only vanilla.

How boring!

I feel sorry for people
who have an easy life,
who don't experience the feeling of overcoming,
of rising to the occasion,
of figuring out a difficult challenge,
of toughing it out,
of persevering,
of bucking up.

Everything is perfect.
Their house is always clean.
Their children are well-behaved
and excelling in school and extracurricular activities.
They enjoy good health.
They don't have financial struggles.

Blah!!

Without adversity,
how would you know what God is capable of?

You would never experience a miracle.

You would never hear God's voice.

How sad.

A Vanilla World: Devotional

And it is impossible to please God without faith.

—Hebrews 11:6 (NLT)

It had been two weeks of hell. Now, being an optimist, I have never said, "Everything that could go wrong, did." But a lot of unpleasant stuff happened all at once.

We had one kid in a hospital in Sacramento, ninety miles away, for a "tune-up." Another one broke her nose and needed surgery to fix it. Another one had a freak asthma attack and was admitted to another hospital in Turlock. Our daughter's car was stolen from in front of our house. A bogus CPS report had been filed on us. It seemed to go on and on.

I had routinely awakened each day and very expectantly said, "Good morning, God! What's up today?" But during this brief time period, my tone of voice changed as I managed to say, with much skepticism, "Hello, God. What on earth can possibly happen today?!"

As Tom and I were passing though our church office on some kind of business or another, Pastor Hanna walked by and nonchalantly asked, "How are things?" Well, we gave him an earful in the thirty seconds he had to listen.

If we expected sympathy, we'd gone to the wrong guy. He smiled and nearly giggled when he said, "It's at such rough times that God can demonstrate His best work!"

Well, I still don't exactly welcome adversity, but I have learned to embrace the message our pastor imparted to us that day. And God has chosen us to experience His miracles on a nearly daily basis. For sure, we feel His presence, which is a miracle in itself, don't you think? The Creator of the entire universe choosing to spend every minute of every day with me—and you.

Join me, when waking up in the morning, in visualizing air moving in and out of our lungs, our bodies functioning in the complex way God made them. Let's marvel at the sunrise and count our many blessings. How can we be anything but grateful? Even if our day holds unknown adversity, we know we are not alone. God is walking along with us, guiding us and providing help along the way in the people He sets to cross our paths.

Dear God,

I love You, and
I love experiencing Your power in my life
on a daily basis.
It would just be nice to have a breather
once in a while.
But I guess You know how much I can take.
I will trust You to handle the details.
Thank You.

Amen.

Our Story:
(Nearly) The End

"You have achieved another all-time low, David." I was looking at his spirometer graph that indicated that his fev1 (lung capacity) fell from 34 percent the previous month to 27 percent today.

"Yippee!" David proclaimed in mock jubilation.

The doctor wasn't amused. He looked up at David and asked, "Is that what you're shooting for, David?"

"No." David felt properly scolded.

"Then what is it you're trying to accomplish?" the doctor inquired with a somber expression.

"Just to stay steady."

"Well, if that's your goal, you're failing."

"You fell seven percentage points in one month," I interjected. "How many more times do you think you can do that and stay alive?"

The doctor didn't give him a chance to answer. "I'll show you. Here is the graph. I'll just complete it." He started to draw on the graph, completing the logical downward trend.

Within moments, he thrust the paper at David. "At this rate, if you don't want to do anything more than what you're doing, you will be in respiratory failure in two months." The doctor's voice was calm but firm.

David and I reacted as if he'd flung a bucket of ice water in our faces.

In my heart of hearts, I had told myself that David probably had a year, two if he was lucky, but *two months*? That could be counted in days!

In complete frustration, the doctor asked, "Well, is there anything more I can do for you, David?"

"No."

"I'll see you next month." He handed David the graph and quickly took his leave.

David and I sat there in stunned silence. I finally walked the two steps across the room and took the paper from David. There it was in black and white—"Respiratory Failure" written in two months' time. David and I were doing the math. He wouldn't be here for Christmas.

My eyes started to tear up, but I tried to keep myself together.

"Is this the way you want things to go, David?"

"Yes."

"You understand what the doctor said? That your lungs won't be able to breathe anymore in two months unless you do more treatments to help them get better?"

"Yes."

"And it's okay with you."

"Yes."

We sat there in silence for a few minutes, wondering what we were supposed to do now.

I finally said, "Is everything good between you and God?"

"Yes."

"Good." My tears started to fall. I found a small box of tissues on the counter and blew my nose. After a few more tense moments, I got up and hugged David. Then I stepped out and asked to talk to the social worker.

When the door closed in the exam room we borrowed, I broke down. I found another little box of tissues and covered my face before dabbing at my eyes and blowing my nose. I was finally able to tell the social worker about the doctor's report. Then I asked for an advance directive.

I went back to wait with David in silence. Finally he said, "I'm not afraid to die. I'm just sad that you are sad."

I just looked at him. "Well, I'm going to miss you, David. You have to know I'll be sad." I blew my nose again.

The social worker came in and had a short talk with David and then left us with the requested forms.

David and I made our way out to the car after a few detours around the inside of the attached buildings. That place is built like a rat's maze!

The drive home was surreal. I cried the whole way but interjected some questions every once in a while.

"Do you want to be buried or cremated?" *Did I just ask my eighteen-year-old son that preposterous question?*

"Whatever is cheapest for you."

Silence for several more miles.

"Do you want to be at home or in the hospital at the end?" *How could I have just asked that? Stop it!*

"I want to be at home."

Good. I wanted that too.

"Except for the last day or two. I don't want to die at home. That way, you won't always walk by and say, 'That was the room David died in.'"

"We wouldn't say that. If you want to be at home, I want you to be there. This is all about what you want."

"Well, I don't even want to sleep in my own bed."

"Why?"

"I already feel as if I'm sleeping with a dead person."

Silence for a few more miles. I wiped my eyes with the palm of my hand and then wiped it on my pants.

I thought about how I would break the news to Tom. I feared he would be angry at David and yell at him, imploring him to do all his prescribed treatments.

I would need to explain to Tom, to convince him this is the path David has chosen. And we have to accept it. We shouldn't spend the last few weeks in battle with him. We simply needed to love him and be with him in whatever capacity he needed us.

I looked over at David, took his hand, and choked out, "I'm not mad at you."

He looked over for just an instant and nodded in understanding. Then we both looked ahead. I kept driving.

As we exited the freeway only a few miles away from home, I said, "We have a decision to make in the next five minutes."

"What's that?"

"We need to decide what to tell your siblings. They're going to see my red eyes and will ask what is the matter."

"Tell them you have allergies."

"That isn't the truth."

"Tell them I went upstairs to clean my room."

"What?"

"In an early episode of the sitcom *Family Matters*, they had another sister. One day, she went upstairs to clean her room and never appeared on the series again."

"Really?"

"Yeah. So you can tell everyone I went upstairs to clean my room. They'll never miss me."

And so began the never-ending round of morbid jokes.

I managed to avoid the kids throughout my dinner preparations. Tom came home from work while I was eating. I called him up to the privacy of our bedroom to tell him the doctor's report. I couldn't say anything before I broke down again. I finally got the words out, and we sat together on the bed and just cried for a few minutes. Then he asked me to call our pastor and Sunday-school teacher to see if they had some time that night to counsel with us. They did, and we left to "run some errands" when we had finished eating.

We shared our dreadful news with our Sunday-school teacher, Smoky Stover, and his wife, Phyl, and then had a few moments of prayer with them. Then we departed and headed to church to meet with our pastor, Dave Kerr. One of his gifts and responsibilities at work was counseling with the bereaved. He was experienced and good at it.

Pastor Kerr advised us to go home right away and tell the other children what the doctor had said. "Actually, it might better if David told them."

Wow, I didn't know if he would be able to, but I was willing to ask him.

We got home after nine o'clock. The younger kids were asleep in bed, as they had school the next day, but Tom got them up while I went to talk with David. He agreed to make the announcement himself. When he finally said the words, "I'm going to die in two months," he had a smile on his face, and the children didn't really believe him.

When we assured them it was true, everyone was silent. Tom made some comments, and then I asked everyone if they had anything to say or had any questions. I could have thrown a shoe at Kelsey when she asked, "Can I have his bedroom?" I guess that was her way of alleviating the tension, but I didn't think it was the least bit funny.

Shannon started to cry. I put my arm around her and pulled her close. McKenna sat across the room, wiping her eyes. I kicked the box of tissues toward her. Even Jordan wiped a tear or two. Then Kelsey asked if the meeting was over, and the little girls said they wanted to go back to bed. I don't know if they really heard what had just been said, but the meeting adjourned.

When the crowd dispersed, I suddenly had a strong desire to have a group hug and to pray together, but the moment had passed, and I couldn't get it back. Instead, I made the rounds, checking on everyone. When I got to Kelsey's and McKenna's room, I found McKenna lying on her top bunk, facing the wall, sobbing. I stood there for a long time, rubbing her back. Then I was called away.

Prayers, Notes, Reflections

8

NEED HELP? LOOK UP!

Heart Psalm 43
Thirteen Clouds on the Ceiling

He lies there, staring at the ceiling.

He sees himself running down field
to catch the football.
He snags it out of the air
and scores the winning touchdown!

Then it's off to the pizza shack.
He eats as much as he wants
without the stigma of swallowing capsules
or the threat of stomach cramps or gas later on.

He and his friends head over to the ice cream parlor.
He lives wildly and tries three new flavors
(without even the thought of pills!).

As they sit and eat and socialize,
the cutest girls flock around him.
They all want to sit by him and talk to him.
They all want to be the lucky one
to wear his letterman jacket.

That evening, instead of spending
an hour and a half on health-related activities,
he checks his e-mail and finds his inbox
is stuffed with messages.
He is, after all, the big man on campus.

He is tall and well-built,
as well as devastatingly handsome and intelligent.

He is in demand in the chat rooms.
All the girls want to go out with him,
and all the boys wish they *were* him.
His future is promising, the sky's the limit!

God, I feel sorry for everyone who isn't me!

Back in his room, while doing his breathing treatments,
he counts the clouds painted on the ceiling.

There are thirteen.

He has been daydreaming again,
about the way life could have been.

If only.

Thirteen Clouds on the Ceiling: Devotional

Blessed is the man who perseveres under trial;
for once he has been approved, he will receive the
crown of life, which the Lord has promised to
those who love Him.

—James 1:12 (NASB)

I painted the upstairs corner bedroom blue. Blue for the
ocean and a lighter blue for the sky. In the ocean were

waves, jumping dolphins, and mermaids with long blonde hair, lounging on rocks near the shore.

One day while I was in that room, David said to me, "There are thirteen clouds on the ceiling."

I had no idea. I had never counted them. I guess he had lain there so many hours, so many days, so many months, staring at the ceiling, probably feeling miserable much of the time. I got to wondering, "What was he thinking about while he was lying there, counting the clouds?"

I began to imagine what I would spend time thinking about if I were David, a teenaged boy who was sick and suffering from a poor body image.

A month before a serious health decline, David had joined a beginning tap dance class. He caught on very fast and loved it, but he could do only a few combinations at a time before he had to step to the side of the room to bend over and cough. It was sad to watch. As we walked to the car after class one week, he said, "It's too bad I couldn't take tap lessons as a well person. I could have been good at this."

If only…

Do you have heartbreaking moments, wondering how life could have been different *if only* your child was healthy? It is a temptation that is best avoided or at least limited. We have to deal with what is, not what we wish was.

> Oh, God!
> My mommy heart breaks!
> I can't help it! I have to ask why.

Why does my child have this disease?
Why couldn't he live the life of a well child?
Things could have been different!
So much better!

Whoa...I lost my head there for a moment,
and I thought I knew better than You.
I'm sorry! Please forgive me.
I trust You. I trust You. I trust You.

Amen.

Heart Psalm 44
Starry-Eyed Love

I wish, I wish for you my child,
time.

Time to experience the
Sweaty-palms,
Leaping-heart,
Goose-pimples,
Can't-wait-to-see-you-again anticipation,
Love-to-hear-your-voice conversations,
Chills-going-down-your-spine,
Starry-eyed love.

Where you caress her neck
and stroke her arm,
and kiss her fingers.
You sit next to her and hold hands,
and it is enough.
But your heart thumps so hard,
and you can't wipe the goofy grin off your face.

Where you drink in the scent of her hair.
The sight of her so breathtaking,
you become drunk just gazing into her eyes.
Where partings are tragically, beautifully painful
and reunions are heavenly.

And she feels exactly the same way about you.

Oh, yes! Hurry, hurry!
Time's a'wastin'!! Go talk to her!
I know, and you know, who your beloved is.
And she likes you, too. I just know it!

Hurry!! Hurry!! Time's a'wastin'!!
There isn't time for bashfulness!
Take a chance!

I pray, I pray for you, my child
to experience starry-eyed love
before it's too late.

Starry-Eyed Love: Devotional

He replied,
"What is impossible for people
is possible with God."

—Luke 18:27 (NLT)

What parent in her right mind would pray that her teenage child would find the love of his life, get married right away, and immediately have a child of his own? Me, that's who.

I guess I might not qualify as being in my right mind, but I long for my sick children to experience true, romantic love, just as I desire that experience for my well children. But time and health are against them.

With sick kids, we find ourselves bending the rules. What is important for some kids, like completing their education and landing that dream job, aren't the all-consuming goals for our sick kids. Tasting from all of life's experiences as quickly as possible has become my goal for them, including marriage, sex, and parenthood (in that order).

I have much to learn regarding surrendering my will and remembering that what God has planned for each of us is beyond my wildest dreams.

What makes me think I know more and am more imaginative than the amazing Creator of the universe? Move over, ego, and make room for the Almighty! God is always at work behind the scenes in ways that astonish me.

But I can trust that He never takes a break. Nothing takes Him by surprise. He has never once hit His forehead with the palm of His hand and exclaimed, "Wow, I didn't see that coming!" or, "Oh, I never thought of that!"

How are you at surrendering your wishes for your sick child to God and His will for him? It's another tough one!

> Dear God,
>
> Please help me trust that You are at work
> in the life of my child.
> Remind me that You love him infinitely more than I do
> and have only good planned for him.
> Even if it doesn't look good to me,
> I must trust that You know more than I do.
> Thank You for Your wisdom and love.
>
> Amen.

Prayers, Notes, Reflections

Heart Psalm 45
Live Your Destiny

Kelsey, David, TJ, McKenna.
Jordan, Shannon, Lynnsey, Nina.
God sent each child for a reason.
Only He knows for what season.

What do you mean? Some are not perfect?
Inherited genetic defect.
Their dad and I, we are to blame?
Sheer disbelief and utter shame.

Life is not fair! is what I felt.
I must live with the hand I'm dealt.
Be of good cheer, please don't despair.
He'll keep us in His loving care.

The road, so hard, with twist and turn.
We each decide what we will learn.
Believe in God, trust and obey.
Just lean on Him, He'll guide the way.

Today is glorious, celebrate!
It may not last, don't hesitate.
Grant me this day just what I need.
My faith is weak, please intercede!

So many strive and work and pray
to find a way to save the day.

But if it is not meant to be,
I must not question Destiny.

Heav'n will one day be the cure.
There, no more treatments to endure.
Imagine life with perfect health,
a dream more cherished than great wealth!

The end of sickness and disease,
to run and play, do as you please
on lush green grass, on streets of gold.
Oh, what a wonder to behold!

Give thanks to God for He is Grand!
He knows what we don't understand.
The how, the why, the final bell...
Fear not, trust God,
love much,
live well!

Live Your Destiny: Devotional

You guide me with your council,
leading me to the glorious destiny.
Who have I in heaven but you?
I desire you more than anything on earth.
My health may fail and my spirit may grow weak,
but God remains the strength of my heart.
He is mine forever.

—Psalm 73:24–26 (NLT)

David always produced more mucus than TJ and McKenna, even when he was little. He always had to do more airway clearance. This is the way it works: He does an albuterol treatment (four times daily) in his nebulizer to open his airways. Next is the nebulized Pulmozyme (once daily), which thins the mucus. Morning and night (on alternate months) is the Tobi, or Colistin, which are inhaled antibiotics to kill the bad bugs living in his lungs. Twice daily, he does the hypertonic saline solution, a nebulized sterile saltwater that irritates the lung lining, which stimulates coughing.

Wearing a percussion vest (the vest replaced manual chest percussion) loosens the mucus, so it will be easier to cough and expel from the body (much like pounding on the bottom of a bottle of ketchup). But that is the secret: coughing and spitting the infected mucus out into the sink, toilet, a tissue, a paper cup, on the ground, in the bushes— take your pick.

But David has always been grossed out by all the nasty things that come out of his diseased body, so he doesn't want to see it (or let others see it). We had great difficulty getting him to comply with the spitting requirement over the years. Besides, David's coughing comes in horrible, choking spasms. It can give him a headache and sometimes causes vomiting. It is exhausting and embarrassing.

So, in essence, David's five hospitalizations in the year 2007 were partly due to his noncompliance. When he swallows his mucus instead of spitting, it fills his stomach and makes him feel full and nauseated. Then he can't eat well. This leads to low energy and ineffective coughing. So his lungs get more infected and produce more mucus, which David coughs and chokes on and swallows. He gets fevers from lung infections and just wants to sleep. He begins to skip his nighttime feeds and loses weight. Eventually, the frustrated mom becomes frantic, calls the doctor, and gets David admitted to the hospital.

Getting our children to do what they need to regardless of their bad body image, despair, and exhaustion is difficult. It is yet another reason we hit the floor with our knees each morning.

> Dear God,
>
> Please teach my child his purpose
> and then help him to live his destiny.
> Thank You, dear God. Amen.

Heart Psalm 46
Living in the Shadow of Death

What do you do when your child's doctor tells you
that your child will likely die in a given period of time,
but he doesn't die?

How do you prepare yourself,
emotionally, for the inevitable
when it turns out not to be imminent?

Do you go on living "normally" (whatever that is)?

Do you make plans?
Help the child set goals for the future?
Prepare their memorial service?

Is it okay to laugh?
To be happy once in a while?

How do you pray?
Do you pray for healing?
For a peaceful ending?
How could I do that?

How many times do you tell your child,
"I love you"
"I'm gonna miss you like crazy"
before they get tired of hearing it?

How many tears
are you allowed to cry?

Who gets the privilege of being present
during the emotional breakdowns?

Meanwhile, the suffering, my child's and mine,
goes on
  and on

      and on

          and on

             and on.

                Will it ever stop?

Please make it stop.

Living in the Shadow of Death: Devotional

Are any of you suffering hardships? You should pray.
Are any of you happy? You should sing praises.
Are any of you sick?
You should call for the elders of the church to
come and pray over you,
anointing you with oil in the name of the Lord.
Such a prayer offered in faith will heal the sick,
and the Lord will make you well.
And if you have committed any sins,
you will be forgiven.
Confess your sins to each other and pray for each
other so that you may be healed.
The earnest prayer of a righteous person has great
power and produces wonderful results.

—James 5:13–16 (NLT)

Did you read every word of the scripture above, or did you just skim it? Did it slap you in the face? Did you want to slap it back? Did it mock you? Did it taunt you? Did you wonder why it may apply to *other* people and *their* children, but not to you and yours?

When our oldest "sick kid" was diagnosed, we held a little healing ceremony at our church for him. We had the pastor anoint our son with oil, we prayed, and we expected him to be healed. We expected a miracle.

When it didn't happen, we waited, and waited, and waited. We kept praying and kept believing. For *years*, we kept vigil. We expected our son's medical tests to prove our miracle had come to pass. We waited for his doctor to say, "You don't need to come see me anymore. Your child is healed. It's a miracle!"

But that never happened. I asked God, "What happened? We were obedient. We did what the Bible said to do. Why didn't you keep up Your end of the bargain?"

What I was eventually able to see and hear is this: God asked me, "Does that scripture mention any time frame?"

I looked and had to admit, "No, it doesn't."

God asked, "Does it mention a location?"

I looked again, and, no, it didn't say, "Pray, anoint with oil, and your child will be healed instantly, on the spot."

But God, in His love and mercy, said to me, "I am faithful. If I don't choose to heal your child here on earth, he will be healed in heaven, where there is no suffering or tears or disease. I know what is best. I have a purpose for everything. Trust Me."

Listen to what God says to you when you ask for an explanation. He will give you the answers you need but not always the ones you want to hear.

> Thank You, dear Lord, for Your loving kindness,
> for Your faithfulness that can be trusted.
> Thank You for my child's healing, whether now or later,
> whether here or in heaven.
>
> Amen.

Heart Psalm 47
Single White Male

SWM seeking a marriage-minded SWF.
Must be a 20- to 25-year-old Christian.
If you desire to enter into a
short-lived relationship
full of bliss
and anguish
with someone who has nothing to offer
in terms of earthly riches
or a long-term future,
please contact me immediately.
Time is of the essence.

Me: I am 23 years old.
I am sick much of the time.
I require a lot of love and care.
I like to eat at McDonald's.
My favorite treats are
Rolos, Junior Mints, and Reese's.
As a percussionist, I love music.
I like to go to the movies, read,
and play video games.
I love God and attending church.
I adore babies
and would like to become a father.
However, I would not be around
to see the child grow up.

So you would have to be willing
to raise the tyke without me.
We will not grow old together
because I will not grow old.
If we hit it off and marry,
I will pledge you my loyalty,
devotion, and affection, and
I will love you
'til the day I die.

Single White Male: Devotional

Don't worry about anything;
instead, pray about everything.
Tell God what you need,
and thank him for all he has done.
Then you will experience God's peace,
which exceeds anything we can understand.
His peace will guard your hearts and minds
as you live in Christ Jesus.

—Philippians 4:6–7 (NLT)

I try to imagine life from behind the eyes of my sick child.
My son is loving, thoughtful, affectionate, and loyal. It
breaks my heart to imagine all that going to waste. I remind
myself that nothing is ever wasted.

What does God have planned for my sick kid? Only He knows.

What feelings and longings does my child experience in the quiet of his heart? Gosh, I wish he chose to share them with me! But maybe I could not bear to know.

What are the yearnings of your sick child? Do you wonder whether God has prepared a special young person to love your child, even if for a short time? What kind of person would enter into a relationship with a chronically or terminally ill person? Would you want your healthy child to love an ill person, knowing heartache is guaranteed in the near future? We can pray for our child and for the person that God may be preparing to enter his life.

> Dear God,
>
> My heart breaks when I think that my son
> likely won't have a long-term future.
> Why, oh, why?
> Please comfort me.
> And please be a friend and a lover to my sick kid,
> who probably won't grow up to experience adulthood
> to the fullest.
> Let him live the abundant life
> in a way I cannot know or imagine.
> Thank You, Lord.
>
> Amen.

Prayers, Notes, Reflections

Heart Psalm 48
That Glorious Day

I took a poll.
I asked my friends
what different ways they know
of saying that someone died.
Here are their responses:

Kicked the bucket, bought the farm,
Passed away, joined the choir invisible,
Entered eternity,
Ceased to be.

Bit the big one, bit the dust,
Checked out, cashed in their chips,
Bought a pine condo, croaked,
Departed.

Taking a dirt nap, gave up the ghost,
Went to a better place, gone to Davy Jones's locker,
Went to meet his maker, passed on,
Expired.

Got whacked, is six feet under,
Got their wings, met the Grim Reaper,
Their number was up, is pushing up daisies,
Fertilizer.

That has got to be a very disrespectful way,
yet a humorous way, to view
such a permanent situation.

But for those of us who know and love Jesus,

we can call it

THAT GLORIOUS DAY!

That Glorious Day: Devotional

That is why we never give up.
Though our bodies are dying,
our spirits are being renewed every day.
For our present troubles are small
and won't last very long.
Yet they produce for us a glory that vastly
outweighs them and will last forever!
So we don't look at the troubles we can see now;
rather, we fix our gaze on things that cannot be seen.
For the things we see now will soon be gone,
but the things we cannot see will last forever.

—2 Corinthians 4:16–18 (NLT)

You may have heard the saying, "This world is not our home, we are just passing through." It is absolutely true! When we are born, our goal is to discover and do God's will, tell others the Good News of Jesus Christ's saving grace, and then go live in heaven for a glorious eternity. It is the much-desired occasion that those who believe the Bible and love Jesus look forward to.

I have known people who kept praying for healing for a very old, very sick person. How many times do they want God to bring healing to that person? More than likely, the sick person longs to go to her permanent home—heaven, where there is no more sickness or disease.

I recently read a book about a preschool-aged child who was deathly ill. During his operation, he visited heaven. I know; you're saying, "Sure he did." But the firsthand account of the details he gave about the things he saw and people he talked to validate his claim. He accurately told of things he'd never learned about and had no knowledge of. You may be comforted to know one thing he said over and over: Jesus really, really loves children!

I don't know about you, but even though I've had a long and strong relationship with Jesus since I was very young, I still harbored 1 percent doubt about the truth of the biblical account of everything we believe. Did Jesus really live and die and rise again? Is he really God? Am I really saved and going to heaven when I die?

I'll bet we all knew people who lived and now are dead. Do you have any idea where they are now? We can think a thing or believe a thing. But can we *know* a thing is absolutely true? What is our alternative? How shall we live?

All I know is this: as I have lived my life for Christ, so many things have happened that have no earthly explanation, that there is no other way to think of it except as divine intervention. A miracle.

Albert Einstein said, "There are two ways to live your life. One is as if nothing is a miracle. The other is as if everything is a miracle." I believe everything is a miracle, from the way our planet's complimentary ecosystems function to the complexity of the human body. I wake up in the morning and feel myself breathe, in and out, and I think it is miraculous. I see the sun in the sky and the flowers and the birds and my children, and I marvel that the earth rotated another time and we did not fly off, considering how fast it is moving through space.

I ponder all these things and know that none of them happened without an intelligent designer. And of what I read about the development of science, I see that the discoveries prove, more and more, everything that is reported in the Bible.

I choose to believe the Bible in its entirety. Therefore, I can believe with a very high degree of certainty that when our children die, they will, indeed, go to a much better place: the arms of our loving Creator and Heavenly Father. That's what it's all about, folks! It's all about That glorious day when all suffering is over and an eternity of true joy will begin!

Dear Lord,

You know we will miss our child.
You experienced that Yourself.
But we trust that You will care for our child
and that we will be reunited with him
at the appointed time.
Thank You forever!

Amen.

And the Beat Goes On

While the three kids were in the hospital around the time of David's eighteenth birthday, a friend of Kelsey's died.

Kelsey was a third grader, and Brianna was a second grader when they met. They were in a multigrade classroom and became fast friends. I met Brianna's mom, Sandy, in December of that school year when the girls had a joint Girl Scout meeting to practice Christmas carols. Sandy and I sat in the back of the room and nursed our babies. I had Jordan, and she had Ryan. They were three weeks apart in age and were about four months old at the time.

Since Brianna sat in a wheelchair due to muscular dystrophy, and I shared with Sandy that I had three kids with health challenges, we found a lot to talk about and became friends. Over the years, we came to rely on one another for support and for a shoulder to cry on when our children were in a medical crisis. We took advantage of many opportunities to have deep, soul-searching conversations about life and death and the meaning of it all.

When I spoke with Sandy on a Wednesday in June of 2007, Brianna had just gone on hospice. I knew you did that only when death was expected in six months or less. She told me that Kelsey had planned a visit with Brianna for that Sunday night. They were going to have a Cirque marathon. They both loved the Cirque du Soleil, and Kelsey was going to bring over several of her DVDs so they could spend time together watching them. I asked Sandy if she thought there was time for Kelsey to wait until Sunday since Kelsey had to work every day until then. I was fishing for information regarding the seriousness of Brianna's condition. Sandy shrugged off the question and said, "I'm pretty sure there's time."

But on that Saturday afternoon, while the rest of our family was at a park in Modesto, waiting for Lynnsey, Shannon, Nina, and me to dance in a recital, my cell phone rang. It was Kelsey. She was sobbing and could hardly talk. She had just gotten a call from Sandy. Brianna had died a couple of hours earlier. She was twenty years old.

Kelsey was heartbroken. She had been planning to see Brianna the next day. She missed visiting with her for the last time by just one day. Our whole family was devastated.

Brianna had spent the night at our house when she was younger, and Kelsey took care of all her needs, including her bathroom and hygiene needs. Kelsey lifted Brianna out of her wheelchair and sat her on the floor so they could play games or watch TV. She would lay her on her bed at night when they went to sleep. She fed and dressed her.

Kelsey also spent many weekends with Brianna and her family over the years. When Kelsey moved away to attend college, they remained close Internet friends.

During Brianna's last week of life and for a couple of weeks following her funeral, Sandy gave me an incredible gift. She and I had some end-of-life conversations that have been very valuable to me. Sandy shared with me the intimate and painful experiences she'd had with Brianna and their family, especially the mechanics and emotions of the last hours and the moment of death. I don't know if it is a common human curiosity, but I needed to hear the details of how a person dies.

I'd had a few conversations with my grandmother and aunt in which they shared with me about the times that they had been with a person at the moment of death, but Sandy shared with me about her own child's death, and it was someone I had known for years. All the while, I couldn't help but relate what she was saying to how it might be when David came to the end.

Sandy and I had walked down a similar path. When she arrived at the end of the road before me, she was gracious enough to share her experiences with me. I think it was good for her to talk about it with me. Many people close to Sandy didn't think she should talk about Brianna because it made her cry. But Sandy told me that the crying was inevitable and a necessary stage of the grieving process. Others wouldn't let her grieve, but I did. I just listened and cried with her, and sometimes I shared some of my memories of Brianna. It helped her very much to know that a lot of people would carry wonderful memories of Brianna in their hearts and that she wouldn't be forgotten.

I shared with Sandy that when I heard the news of Brianna's death, I was at the very stadium where Kelsey and

I had watched Brianna graduate from eighth grade. And I told her that when Nina heard that Brianna died, she said, "That's so sad. I remember sitting on her lap and dancing with her in her wheelchair. She was really nice."

Those are the kinds of memories I would want someone to share with me about my child if I were in the same situation. And I think it warmed Sandy's heart to hear them.

She told me things I will need to store away for a while. I always wondered how a parent could continue to live after the death of a child. When I voiced my thoughts to Sandy, she said, "You don't know how you keep going, but you just do, especially when you have other children to care for. You find a way to get up in the morning. You manage to take another bite of food to keep yourself going. You pray for strength, and it comes."

It's comforting to have someone I love and trust guiding me down the path I am traveling on. Sandy's friendship is a gift from God. He is the One we both rely on to get us through the struggles of life, and He is the One who comforts us.

Every life experience is from God and has a purpose. As the saying goes, "Life is about the journey, not the destination." I truly believe it's about both. I want to make it a journey well traveled, and I desperately desire all my children to come to this understanding also.

I recently attended a funeral for an elderly woman from our church. One of the messages shared by a dear friend of hers stuck in my head. It was from a vacation they had taken together. The elderly woman had gotten up early each day and was dressed and downstairs with everyone else even though she could have slept a while longer. Her companions asked her, "What are you doing up so early?" Her answer: "I didn't want to miss a thing!"

That is how I feel. I don't want to miss a thing. And I don't want my children to miss a thing. I am learning that I am power*less* to make it all happen, but God is power*ful* to make happen what is supposed to happen. It's all about trust and acceptance. All of life is either a blessing or a lesson. My days are full of both blessings and lessons. They are painful at times, but they are also joy-filled. And I don't want to miss any of it! I hope you don't either!

God sends comfort to each of us in our quiet moments. Often it is in the form of friends and family members at much-needed times. Let's make sure our hearts are open to recognize His comfort, accept it, and express our gratitude for it. Let us all comfort one another when our paths cross as we journey together, raising our chronically ill children.

The

H

A

R

D

Y

C

H

I

L

D

R

E

N

2002

AFTERWORD

MUSIC AND MAYHEM

ONE OF MY friends, who looked over an early edition of my manuscript, suggested that the readers might want a fuller picture of our children's lives. She has known our family for nearly fifteen years and has seen the children grow and blossom in their extracurricular pursuits. She wanted you, the reader, to know more of our children besides that which is health-related. The following is my attempt to fulfill her wish:

For the first twenty-five years of our marriage, we believed ourselves to be "baby people," not "animal people." But slowly, for a variety of reasons, we have adopted wayward and needy dogs, cats, and a potbellied pig. The number fluctuates month to month as some expire and others wander onto our property, needing care. Currently, we have five cats, two dogs, and one pig. They are all loved and are therapeutic to us in different ways. We all find joy in caring for our much-loved pets and are loved and entertained by them in return. And due to the fact that I eat a lot of eggs as my primary protein source since becoming a vegetarian, we have also acquired twelve chickens under the agreement that *I'll feed them if they feed me.*

Some of the activities our children have been involved in over the years, besides school, are sports and music. They have been in gymnastics, swimming, karate, tennis, and two or three summers of soccer. Five of the children were on a competitive city track team for four or five years.

I have a habit of second-guessing my every decision. I rarely know whether my parenting is effective or whether I am doing the right thing. But one thing I know: music has always spoken to me and aided in healing the hurt places. It touches a place down in my soul and helps me get in touch with hidden feelings. I wanted to pass that along to my children, if possible. So the following is what has ensued. I am grateful that God has blessed all our children with talent in the music and performing arts. When people say some of our children shouldn't have been born, I look at the kids and their accomplishments and how they bless this world. Then I can ignore the naysayers.

Even though my husband, Tom, has two college degrees, he does not work in his chosen field. He has sacrificed his dream of working as a photographer all these years so he could support his family and obtain those all-important medical benefits. For most of our kids' childhoods, Tom has been a truck driver. With the economy the way it is, we are grateful that he is employed and healthy enough to work. Because of his sacrifice, I have been able to stay home (although I am rarely at home) and participate in our children's lives on a daily basis. Thank you, honey! A new chapter opened up for Tom as he fulfilled a lifelong desire to learn to ride a motorcycle. Much to my chagrin, he purchased a bike in 2014 and will use any excuse to go out riding, including his short commute to and from work. He absolutely loves riding!

I took violin lessons for four years, beginning in elementary school. My orchestra teacher encouraged me to quit (I wasn't very good) and join the choir in junior high. So I did. One day while in high school, I heard the marching band practicing. It excited me so much, I said, "I've got to do that!" But since I was musically challenged, I wondered what I could do. I found a way: try out for the drill team! I did and I made it! I marched in parades with the Newark High School Marching Band for my junior and senior years of school, carrying one of the letters of our school name in front of the band. I sang in the high school choir and also in college at Ohlone Community College, and I competed on the gymnastic and badminton teams at Newark High.

I began performing in summer musicals in Modesto in 2007 and have done two shows per summer ever since. At age 46, I began three years of tap and one year of ballet, jazz, and worship dance classes. I even took eight dance classes per week in preparation for one of the summer shows. What a blast! (No, I didn't get the role. I was too old.)

Sometime around the year 2005, my grandmother came to live in our town, and I became her caregiver, and shortly after, my aunt came to live with Grandma, so I began caring for her, also. In 2014, I started acting in films in Los Angeles. It was a great way to spend extra time with McKenna, who also acted in LA, and also bring in a little bit of extra money (very little!). Around that time, I also became employed as our church wedding hostess and shortly after, I became a member of the board of directors for Modesto Performing Arts.

McKenna and I made the decision to suspend our acting in Southern California in the late winter of 2016 due to David's declining health. We felt the need to be closer to home for this last chapter in his life. It caused David great distress having us three hundred miles away from Modesto for even one day, so he felt much comfort and security having us home for now.

I joined church choirs over the years, and I married a guy who could sing and play the guitar. I was overjoyed when we began having children who all displayed musical talent. All the kids sang with our church children's choir and performed in the Easter and Christmas musicals. And when they were old enough, they took music lessons in their public schools.

Kelsey began playing the clarinet in fifth grade and played on into college. She also picked up the saxophone and percussion instruments, marching with a big bass drum one year and traveling cross-country to compete in percussion competitions. In high school (Modesto High), she auditioned for and won spots in the county honor band more than once. Kelsey began performing in musicals with Modesto Performing Arts (MPA) during the summer of 2011 and continued with her acting with several other companies and churches. She played her clarinet and sang in the local college programs and played the clarinet in the summer band in the park. She was a deacon at our church and was a junior high leader in the youth department until she moved away from home. Kelsey graduated from Modesto Junior College and went on to earn her BA in psychology from San Francisco State University in the spring of 2016. She has traveled to several islands in the Caribbean and other countries and loves discovering the people and landscapes of distant places.

David began his music career in fifth grade when his grandfather taught him to play the recorder. They played a few duets at Tom's parents' fiftieth wedding anniversary party. This thrilled me because wind instruments are good for kids with cystic fibrosis, since blowing in the instruments exercises their lungs. But David settled on percussion instruments as his main contribution to many groups over the years, including Trade Winds Dance Band, where he became a paid professional. This includes the drum set, mallet instruments like marimbas and vibraphones, as well as three handbell ensembles. He also played for the county honor band. David performed onstage in a musical (MPA) during the summer of 2011, and he played percussion instruments in the college band. He played percussion in our church praise band. David received percussion awards in junior high and high school and the "unsung hero" and rookie awards for Modesto High. Sadly, David had to retire from his musical performing groups during the summer of 2013 due to his declining health. He became dependent on oxygen in early 2016 but has kept a cheerful disposition and enjoys the company of our pets and his siblings. When David was 18 years old, he moved out of our house into a house shared by three other guys until one of the guys stole all the rent money, and the electricity was turned off, preventing David from doing his breathing treatments. He then found a room in a large apartment with a vacancy and lived there for a year until he needed to be hospitalized. Upon his release, he moved back home, where he enjoys his independence in the "boys' house" but has family close by to help out when needed.

TJ began playing clarinet and even marched one year in the high school marching band before he settled in the pit, playing percussion. He also joined the church hand bell ensemble. Then he learned that he enjoys singing. He joined four singing groups at the junior college and church when he was twenty years old and auditioned for musical stage plays (MPA). He performed in four shows during the second half of 2011 and two musicals during the summer of 2012 and has had featured dance roles and solo parts each summer since. TJ loves to sit down and tinkle around at the piano, even though he hasn't had formal lessons. The women at church love to hear TJ play for them as they cook and set the tables for the weekly dinners. In the fall of 2012, TJ auditioned for and joined the Modesto Symphony Orchestra (MSO) Chorus. TJ volunteered at church as a gardener, is a barista at the coffee cart, and taught adult Sunday school. TJ is studying to earn a certificate in graphic arts. He played ukulele in a group until he became a member of a barbershop chorus, which rehearsed on the same night of the week.

McKenna began playing the flute in fifth grade and quickly developed her talent to the point that she played solos in high school and with the county honor band. She marched for three years and became the marching band's drum major for two years. She also sang with the elite chamber ensemble in high school, as well as the honor choir in junior high and high school and on into college. She was awarded a high honor from the Modesto High staff for courage in the face of adversity. She auditioned for a new youth handbell group in town and got in when she was in seventh grade. She rang handbells in our church ensemble until she had a scheduling conflict. She also taught herself to play the guitar and fiddles around on piano. McKenna worked backstage with community stage productions, building sets, sewing costumes, and moving scenery during shows. But in the summer of 2011, she began appearing on stage in musicals (MPA) with six members of her family. In 2012, McKenna began modeling and acting professionally. She appeared in a Chevy Chase movie (Lovesick) and made an AT&T commercial with Victoria Justice, as well as staring in a student film and many other projects in the following years. McKenna played tennis in college as well as learned yoga, weightlifting, martial arts, and aerobics to aid in her health. She represented Canada (as a descendent of a Canadian) in a beauty pageant in January of 2013. She tries to be a full-time college student, but her health keeps sidetracking her, and she, occasionally, has to drop her classes when she gets sick. She had decided on majoring in nutrition but switched to interior design. She worked part time in a clothing store and has plays solos and duets (flute) at church and was a youth group volunteer.

Jordan began trumpet lessons in the fifth grade and played for six years. During his junior high and high school years, he also learned to play the baritone, percussion instruments like the marimba, the guitar, ukulele, and handbells. He was a featured singer in junior high and high school choirs and ensembles. Jordan was drum major for one year with McKenna, but then he quit band and choir so he could perform with the drama department and run cross-country. He has performed in talent shows with a dance production group and in the concert and marching percussion group. He began his modeling career in San Francisco and Fresno at age 16. He played feature roles in musicals at his high school, a community group (MPA), our church, and a neighboring church for five years. (Look for him on YouTube.) Jordan is a gifted songwriter and woos the girls with his ukulele while singing his songs. He received band and choir awards in junior high. Jordan sang in our church youth praise band until he joined the US Marine Corps in August of 2012, where he is proudly serving our great country. He has excelled in his training, become a respected leader, traveled to several countries around the world, and plans to return to the states and pursue other interests, perhaps in the medical field, when he has fulfilled his obligation.

Shannon began playing piano in third grade and violin in fourth. She picked up the saxophone in fifth grade and was a valued and dedicated member of the junior high band and high school marching band (getting permission to begin high school band competitions as a junior high student). She has participated in her junior high and high school honor choir. In junior high, she performed on stage in a musical with a community youth company (YES Company). Shannon took dance lessons for two years and piano for three. She also rang handbells in our church ensemble until she had a scheduling conflict with the band practices. Shannon's piano lessons came in handy as she played keyboard in the high school percussion group as they performed in competitions. She also played many percussion instruments for two years in the high school band and percussion group. Shannon volunteered at church working with the babies and toddlers until she graduated high school and took a job in the kitchen of a Christian camp near Yosemite.

Lynnsey began playing violin in elementary school, received private piano lessons at home, and then settled on the trumpet for fifth through seventh grade. As an eighth grader, she was allowed to compete with the high school marching band, playing percussion instruments, just like Shannon. So her junior high band teacher had her play percussion in the junior high school band. Lynnsey has performed in community musical plays (MPA and YES kids) and sang with her junior high choir. She took three years of tap dance lessons and was awarded the choir award in both seventh and eighth grade. She sang in the high school advanced choir, competed in the all-state honor choir and played percussion in the high school band. Lynnsey did some modeling but took an ROP course at the hospital in her junior year of high school and decided to go into nursing. Lynnsey competed with the color guard during winter season during her senior year of high school.

Nina began piano lessons at age 4 and continued for three years. In fourth grade, she took violin lessons at school and then switched to flute in fifth grade. She sang in her elementary school choir and took ballet lessons for six years. She also took tap and jazz for several years. Nina has performed in many community productions (MPA, YES kids), as well as eleven church musicals at both our church and a neighboring church. In the musicals, she had dance and vocal solos. She continued to take choir and band classes in junior high school, where she was a valued pit player in the Modesto High School Marching Band, as an eighth grader. Nina became a member of the Performing Arts Academy at Modesto High during her sophomore year. Nina has also modeled but is entertaining the idea of becoming a pilot in the US Air Force.

As you might imagine, we are all busy. I spent much of my time driving our children and many of their friends from one rehearsal to another in our fifteen-passenger van until it pooped out a couple of years ago. The logistics can get tricky, but I love every minute of it! It is getting a bit easier now that the kids are growing up and becoming a bit more independent.

I love watching a show progress from auditions, through rehearsals, and end at the performances. I love hearing the different groups rehearse. I also enjoy taking my one-hundred-year-old blind grandma to all the concerts. December and May are particularly busy, with all the holiday and end-of-the-school-year concerts, but I love it all—except, that is, when the schools double-book. Then Tom and I have to divide and conquer. There have been times when one of us saw one child play in the band or sing a solo but missed another child receive an award at the other concert. Oh, well, that's what cameras are for!

Two things have saved our family and held it together over the years: our faith in God and music. Music, which God invented, has healing powers like no medicine I know of. A few years ago, when David was dreadfully ill, his music classes were the only things that could get him out of bed. The high school marching band has become our third family, the second being our church family. We spent/spend so much time with that group of children and booster parents that we feel like family. I know our children will count some of their band buddies as lifelong friends.

Moving to a large property with two houses, a huge patio, and a swimming pool at the beginning of 2010 has opened a new wonderful chapter in our lives. Our family's ministry expanded to having cast parties, choir parties, band parties, youth parties, and just any old excuse to have people over to share our blessings. We have bonfires in the fire pit, roast marshmallows, cook hot dogs and hamburgers on the big outdoor barbecue grill, and have tons of fun with all our honored guests.

Well, I hope you have enjoyed getting to know our family a bit more. And I hope you have been inspired to discover the healing power that music and especially a relationship with God can have on your life. I encourage you to seek out, support, and participate in community musical programs and to look for a Bible-believing church to get involved with. They will become your second family and your strongest supporters during your times of great need.

David, TJ
& McKenna
Three Siblings
With Cystic Fibrosis

The Hardy Family

March 2016

Appendix

Medical Terminology

I DEFINED THESE terms myself so nonmedical persons could understand them. They are not definitions from a medical book. The terms may also have other meanings or applications, but I am relating them to our family's experience.

Advair: Premeasured dose of powdered medication to be inhaled. (Tastes terrible.)

Albuterol: Liquid that is vaporized in a nebulizer to be breathed over twenty to thirty minutes. Opens air passages. (Bronchodilator.)

amylase, protease, lipase: Three enzymes produced in the pancreas to digest food.

antibiotics: Medication to combat infection.

Bilirubin: Substance that can become elevated in the body if not washed away by the kidneys.

catheter: Tube inserted into the urethra to drain away urine.

celiac disease: Allergies to many foods, including wheat.

CFRD: Cystic fibrosis–related diabetes.

clubbed fingers: Fingernails and toenails are flatter and thicker in people with CF than other people. The worse the lung damage, the worse the clubbing.

Colistin: Antibiotic that is nebulized into a vapor and breathed to combat lung infections. (Tastes terrible.)

concussion: Can happen in a person with a head injury. It can be mild or very serious.

Cystic Fibrosis: Inherited, genetic illness primarily affecting the respiratory and digestive systems.

DNA: Building block of the human body. It is found in every cell. (Deoxyribonucleic acid.)

endoscopy: Procedure in which a tiny camera is passed through the mouth and down the throat to take pictures of the patient's stomach. Patient is usually sedated.

enema: Medication inserted through the rectum to clean all fecal matter from the colon.

enzymes: Capsules containing amylase, protease, and lipase to aid in digestion.

exocrine system: Every place in the body that makes sweat and mucus, as well as other substances.

G-tube: Gastrostomy tube is surgically inserted from the outside of the belly into the stomach and is used to pump extra nutritional formulas and/or medications.

genotype: In-depth look into the details of a person's genes to determine whether she has a disease or condition.

gestational diabetes: Diabetes a pregnant woman has only during the pregnancy.

hospice: Organization that offers spiritual and medical support to families and patients when the patient is not expected to live more than six months.

IV: Medication is pumped into a patient through a needle that is (usually) inserted into a vein in the hand or arm.

insulin: Substance produced in the pancreas; needed to regulate blood sugar.

jaundice: Condition that can happen in newborns and other people when their kidneys aren't functioning properly.

lung bleed: A blood vessel in the lung bleeds and can result in death within a few minutes if it doesn't seal itself.

Make-a-Wish: Nonprofit organization dedicated to fulfilling a wish of children who have a fatal illness.

manual chest therapy: pounding (clapping) on a patient's chest, sides, and back in different positions to loosen thick mucus to be coughed and spat out.

meningitis: Brain infection.

nebulizer: Small machine that vaporizes liquid medication to be inhaled by patient.

NICU: Neonatal intensive care unit.

pancreas: Organ of the digestive system; enzymes and insulin are made here.

percussion vest: Vest that inflates and then percusses the lungs to loosen mucus. Replaces manual chest therapy.

PICC line: Long-term IV that is inserted in the inner upper arm, threaded up the vein and around the shoulder, and ends near the heart. Lasts one to two weeks.

portacath: Surgically implanted device that aids in very long term IV medications. Ideally, can last up to ten years. Usually implanted in the upper side of the chest or middle inside of the arm.

Pulmozyme: Inhaled medication developed to thin mucus in the lungs.

schizophrenia: Mental illness.

spinal tap: Procedure in which fluid is taken from the lower spine.

sweat test: Diagnostic tool used to determine the sweat chloride level in a patient. High levels indicate CF.

Tobi: Inhaled antibiotic.

Tourette syndrome: Condition that causes body ticks and verbal outbursts.

vas deferens: Part of the male reproductive system that can be damaged in persons with CF.

Resource List

American Heart Association, Inc.
205 East 42nd Street
New York, NY 10017
(212) 661-5335

American Diabetes Association
1660 Duke
Alexandria, VA 22314
1-800-232-3472

American Cancer Society
777 Third Avenue
New York, NY 10036

American Lung Association
1740 Broadway
New York, NY 10019
(212) 315-8700

The Arthritis Foundation
115 East 18th Street
New York, NY 10003
(212) 477-8700

Association for the Care of Children's Health
7910 Woodmont Avenue
Suite 300
Bethesda, MD 20814

Cancer Care, Inc.
The National Cancer Foundation, Inc.
One Park Avenue
New York, NY 10016
(212) 221-3300

Cystic Fibrosis Research, Inc (CFRI)
2672 Bayshore Parkway, Suite 520
Mountain View, CA 94043
Tel: 650.404.9975; Fax: 650.404.9981
For general information: cfri@cfri.org

Cystic Fibrosis Foundation (CFF)
Cystic Fibrosis Foundation (national headquarters)
6931 Arlington Road, 2nd floor
Bethesda, Maryland 20814
info@cff.org

Epilepsy Foundation of America
4351 Garden City Drive
Landover, MD 20785

Lupus Foundation of America, Inc.
4 Research Place
Suite 180
Rockville, MD 20850-3226

Multiple Sclerosis National Society
205 East 42nd Street
New York, NY 10017
(212)986-3240

National Hospice Organization
1901 North Fort Myer Drive
Suite 902
Arlington, VA 22209
(703) 243-5900

National Kidney Foundation
2 Park Avenue
New York, NY 10016
(212) 887-2210

Stroke Foundation, Inc.
898 Park Avenue
New York, NY 10021
(212) 734-3461

Suggested Reading List

Books I have learned from in no particular order:

The Shack by William P. Young
Published in 2007
Wind Blown Media
ISBN-10: 160941411X

Parenting Children with Health Issues by Lisa Green
with Dr. Foster Cline
Copyright 2007
Published by The Love and Logic Press
The Love and Logic Institute
2207 Jackson St. Suite 102
Golden, Colorado 80401-2300
ISBN-10: 1930429894
www.loveandlogic.com

Alive at 25 by Andy Lipman
Copyright 2001 by Andy Lipman
Published by LONGSTREET PRESS, INC.

2974 Hardman Court
Atlanta, CA 30305
ISBN-10: 1563526816

Sick Girl Speaks by Tiffany Christiansen
Copyright 2007
iUniverse
2021 Pine Lake Road, Suite 100
Lincoln, NE 68512
ISBN-10: 059547201X

A Purpose Driven Life by Rick Warren
Copyright 2002
Published by Zondervan
ISBN-10: 0310334195

The Power of Two by Isabel Stenzel Byrnes and Anabel Stenzel
Copyright 2007 by
The curators of the University of Missouri
University of Missouri Press, Columbia, Missouri 65201
ISBN-10: 0826217540

It's Good to be Alive by Jack Rushton
Published 2010
Published by Cedar Fort, Inc.
ISBN-10: 1599554089

Heaven is for Real by Todd Burpo
Published 2010
Thomas Nelson Publishers
ISBN-10: 0849946158

When Is it Right to Die? By Joni Eareckson Tada
Copyright 1992 by Joni Eareckson Tada
Zondervan Publishing House
Grand Rapids, Michigan 49530
ISBN-10: 0756786894

The Spirit of Lo by Terry and Don Detrich
Copyright 2000, 2003 Terry and Don Detrich
Mind Matters, Inc.
P.O. Box 52503
Tulsa, Oklahoma 74152-0503
ISBN-10: 0970193408
www.spiritoflo.com

Blow the House Down by Charles Tolchin
Copyright 2000 by Charles Peter Tolchin
Published by Writers Club Press
An imprint of iUniverse.com, Inc.
620 North 48th Street Suite 201
Lincoln, NE 68504-3467
ISBN-10: 0595005586
www.iuniverse.com

Breathing Room
The Art of Living with Cystic Fobrosis
A Collection of Stories
A Project By Michelle Compton
www.thebreathingroom.org

The New Evidence That Demands a Verdict
By Josh McDowell
Thomas Nelson; Rev Upd edition (November 23, 1999)
ISBN-10: 0785242198

ABOUT THE AUTHOR

KATHY HARDY WAS raised in Newark, California, and moved to Modesto in the year 2000. She has always enjoyed writing and, as an adult, found that daily journaling served as therapy for the many tremulous events surrounding the diagnosis and care of her children. Kathy has been married to Tom for thirty-five years. Together they are raising their eight beautiful, talented, and intelligent children, surrounded by music and mayhem. All the children sing, dance, play multiple instruments, model, act, and perform in many ensembles, companies, groups, and bands around Stanislaus county and beyond. To spend more time with her children, Kathy performs in two musical productions with them each summer and does some acting in Los Angeles with a couple of them. She also works in her garden (an acre and a half), enjoys reading, and takes care of their numerous cats, dogs, chickens, and "Miss Piggy," their potbellied pig. Her faith and church involvement are the bedrock of her existence. She sings in her church choir and attends Bible study, is a board member at a local theater company, is a caregiver for her elderly aunt and one-hundred-year-old blind grandmother, and is the wedding hostess at her church. Kathy also makes appearances and gives inspirational talks to special groups.

Contact the author:
E-mail at kathy-hardy@att.net
Visit the author at www.kathyhardy.com.

CPSIA information can be obtained at www.ICGtesting.com
Printed in the USA
LVOW10s0454310816

502538LV00014B/84/P

9 781683 522157